Edinburgh Bilingual Library (5)

EDINBURGH BILINGUAL LIBRARY (5)

Anthology of
Contemporary French Poetry

EDITED AND TRANSLATED BY
GRAHAM DUNSTAN MARTIN
Lecturer in French
University of Edinburgh

UNIVERSITY OF TEXAS PRESS, AUSTIN

International Standard Book Number 0–292–71006–2
Library of Congress Catalog Card Number 78–38574
Copyright © 1971 by Edinburgh University Press
All rights reserved

Printed in the United States of America

Second Printing 1975

Edinburgh Bilingual Library

FOREWORD

An imperfect knowledge of a language need be no bar to reading a work written in it if there is a good translation to help. This Library may aid those who have a wide-ranging and adventurous interest in literature to jump the hurdles of language and thus do something to help break down the barriers of specialization. That it may be helpful for courses in Comparative Literature is our hope, but not our main aim. We wish to appeal to a wider audience: first to the cultivated, serious reader of literature who is not content to remain within the English language, secondly to university students and teachers of English and of Modern Languages by inviting them to throw from outside some new light on, perhaps even discover different values in, their particular fields of specialization.

As this Bilingual Library grows it will try to map, in a necessarily limited and modest way, small areas of Western Literature through the comparison of actual texts. This it will do by building up groups of volumes to illustrate literary traditions, themes and styles. Thus No. 3, *Troubadour Lyric Poetry*, will be followed by volumes of *Minnesang*, Petrarch, Ausias March and others, which together will chart the range and significance of Courtly Love. From time to time volumes will be paired to show literary development across countries and periods. Thus, the technical and conceptual development in the reworking of classical mythology will be shown by the simultaneous publication of Poliziano's *Orfeo* and Góngora's *Polifemo*—the one at the beginning, the other at the end, of the Age of Humanism.

The languages represented will be French (with Provençal),

German, Italian, Portuguese, Russian, Spanish (with Catalan), and Medieval and Renaissance Latin. The translations will not be 'cribs' but good literature worth publishing in its own right. Verse will be translated into verse, except where the unfamiliarity of the language for most readers (Provençal, Catalan, Old French, Old High German) may make a more literal prose rendering advisable. In the majority of cases the Introductions will present up-to-date assessments of each author or work, or original interpretations on a scholarly level. Works already accessible in translation will only be included when we think we can offer new translations of special excellence.

A. A. Parker
GENERAL EDITOR

Contents

Anthology of
Contemporary French Poetry

INTRODUCTION

The main concern of this anthology is to present what I take to be the most interesting new figures in French poetry of the 1950s and 60s. I have therefore, and with much regret, omitted many of the best-known and older poets still writing, in favour of younger and lesser-known ones. Thus, to mention only the most important omissions, I have left out the present grand old man of French poetry, Pierre Jean Jouve, along with Saint-John Perse, Henri Michaux, Francis Ponge, René Char and Pierre Emmanuel, all of whom are well-established figures. I have, however, tried to balance contemporaneity against quality: the difficulty here is that, contrary to popular belief, poets do not usually publish really significant work much before their middle thirties. Consequently only two poets represented here were born after 1939. Some trends, such as concrete poetry, I have excluded by deliberate policy. But of such omissions, something will be indicated in the pages that follow, as I endeavour to map out the main currents, and indicate their sources.

One major source is of course the Surrealists, who are still in being as a coherent group, but no longer dominate the poetic scene as they did between the wars. By World War II, indeed, most of its finest writers had left the movement, and it is now very much a minor coterie. It is represented here mainly by Joyce Mansour and Jean-Pierre Duprey, who illustrate two of its salient characteristics: the dredging of frankly sexual and obsessive imagery from the unconscious, and (in Duprey's case) a lively verbal technique resembling free association. Surrealism offered its practitioners a kind of theory and practice of inspiration. By such techniques as automatic writing the image-forming abilities of a writer's unconscious were, in theory, liberated. The resulting texts were often in large part incomprehensible to the conscious mind. But connexions were assumed to exist in the unconscious: *it* would understand, even if the intelligence remained baffled. As André Masson observes, the practice of automatic writing is like the sport of fishing: you may take home a fat trout, or you may pull in an old boot. And since both forethought and afterthought were in theory frowned on, and form was usually the effect of hazard or momentary choice, the effectiveness of surrealist poems depends almost solely upon their imagery: to convince, they need to achieve an irresistible flow of passion, colour and energy. This can be seen occurring in the work of Aimé Césaire, who was at one time connected with the Surrealists, and whose style seems to be 'naturally' surrealistic.

Surrealism appeared to dominate French poetry between the wars. But after 1945 it became apparent that there were other major figures lurking in the background, who had not been given or who may not even have sought a hearing, and whose concerns, though completely 'modern', were of a quite different sort. Neither Saint-John Perse nor Pierre Jean Jouve, for instance, really became known until after the War. And, difficult though they are, the intellect is firmly in control in the work of both. Pierre Jean Jouve for example believes as firmly in the power of the unconscious as any Surrealist, for he was profoundly influenced by his involvement in a Freudian case-history in the 1930s. But though he claims to obtain his images from the unconscious, he regards his poems as organisms, each having its own inbuilt system, exercises very tough intellectual control over them, and often uses a fairly strict form. Among those influenced by him directly, one can mention the Canadian poet Fernand Ouellette, and Jean Paul Guibbert. The main point is, however, that Surrealist-type 'frenzy' and inspiration are out of fashion, and that the thinking mind has returned to the French poem. Garelli is a staunch defender of surrealistic imagery, it is true; but this defence is offered in the name of reason.[1] And this is symptomatic of a general change of attitude.

Among poets born in the 1920s, Yves Bonnefoy has doubtless the biggest reputation. And his poetry can be seen as a special type of reaction against Surrealism and in favour of the intellect. Where Surrealism had been instinct with colour, fantastic imagery, and a vocabulary drawn from all spheres of experience, Bonnefoy seeks puritanically to reduce colour to a minimum, and confines his vocabulary to a few elemental symbols. Where Surrealism denied the validity of all literary and poetic values, Bonnefoy seeks a new classicism, and rejects what he defines as 'unpoetic'. His poetry is based upon a personal theory of language, which is worth a few pages' serious consideration: for, if he is right, translation from French into English presents the translator with an insoluble problem; and even the English speaker who reads French is, I suspect, not seeing the original French poem, but an anglicized shadow of it cast by his own Anglo-Saxon mind.

The problem is perhaps connected with the famous 'clarity' traditionally attributed to the French language. Clarity we may take to signify a meaning which the rational mind finds unambiguous. This can be achieved in two ways. Words can be applied to particular objects, in the form perhaps of a meticulous description; but then language will become too precise, will not carry enough overtones, to reverberate in the mind: it will become scientific, not poetic. Or else words can be divorced (as far as is possible) from particular individual realities (particular stones, trees, flowers), and used to refer to abstract categories, those universal qualities supposedly discernible behind all particular instances. The result is, in a sense, an ambiguity (because when analysed, it yields a diversity) which is unambiguous (because it includes within it all its own diversity). If 'fire', for instance, refers in a text to all varieties of the phenomenon (both physical and emotional) we call 'fire', then it is ambiguous in that it has a multiplicity of particular references, unambiguous in that it comprehends them all. If this policy is followed, words come to be used in a 'universal', non-concrete sense, as if referring to a world of essences, of Platonic *ideas*.

Thus, in Eluard's lines:

Je fis un feu, l'azur m'ayant abandonné,
Un feu pour être son ami,
Un feu pour m'introduire dans la nuit d'hiver,
Un feu pour vivre mieux.
[I made a fire, for the azure had abandoned me,
A fire to be her friend,

A fire to enter the winter night,
A fire to live better.]

'fire' and 'azure' are, in their emotional senses, so ambiguous
as to be capable of any acceptable emotional interpretation:
the meaning of 'fire' can range from mere 'comfort' or 'con-
solation', through warmer emotions, to what we call a 'burn-
ing passion'. And all these interpretations are doubtless
intended simultaneously. The image thus achieves the curious
and characteristically Eluardian effect at once of great ambigu-
ity and suggestiveness, and of great apparent clarity and purity.
'Fire' and 'azure' take on an almost elemental quality.

Now, according to Bonnefoy, words are not only *used* in
French as if they referred to Platonic 'ideas': this is how they
are most commonly *felt*. He calls this the 'principle of identity':
French words seem to coincide not with appearances but with
entities, and abstractions are felt as substances.[2] Bonnefoy's
Lieu de la Salamandre, as he himself has pointed out, does not
start, as a poem by Hopkins or Ted Hughes would, with
concrete particulars, but uses words like 'fire', 'stone', 'heart',
'death', words which in short are capable of being felt as
'essences' or archetypes, words which Bonnefoy thinks draw
our contemplation to the threshold of life and death, and have
implicit in them the problems of being and non-being. Accord-
ing to him, the more explicit words, such as 'leaves' or 'night-
ingales', have, in French (unlike in English) lost their sacred
associations. He therefore prefers 'pierre' to 'brique', 'silex'
to 'silicate', 'crier' and 'rire' to 'grimacer' and 'ricaner' ('stone'
to 'brick', 'flint' to 'silicate', 'shout' and 'laugh' to 'grimace'
and 'snigger').[3] A poetry of essences is thus, he thinks, forced
upon the French writer who desires as 'high' and 'pure' a
poetry as possible.

In English poetry, then, universals are reached through a
hard outer surface of sense-data; but in French poetry the
effort to universalize the poem often leads it to avoid all but
the most general direct reference. The images may in a sense
be concrete, but in a general kind of way: as in *Lieu de la
Salamandre*, they have no particularity, and their references
become bewilderingly wide. If, as in the Eluard poem quoted
above, 'azur' and 'feu' can stand for so much, the very multi-
plicity of their senses can suggest not only plenitude, but also
nothingness: they are both full and empty of meaning, and

Paradise becomes equated with Nirvana. But this is precisely Bonnefoy's intention: he wishes poetry to concern itself with 'being'; he intends to bring the reader face to face with the problems of 'being' and 'non-being'. His own poetry is not so much about particular experiences as an attempt to 'conjurer le vrai fruit dans le fruit sensible, évoquer dans une saveur la saveur de l'unité que l'on cherche.' [to conjure the true fruit out of the physical fruit, to evoke from a flavour the flavour of the unity we seek.] He does not build up an interlocking web of meanings which in turn suggest a universal, but tries to suggest a 'presence', a 'reality', a privileged awareness *directly*.

Now there is a whole school of post-war French poets who have either followed Bonnefoy's example or found very similar solutions for themselves. Exemplars of this 'school' are du Bouchet, Dupin, Jean Laude and Roger Giroux. And Jean Paris's anthology of 1956 is mainly devoted to poets who adopt this style of language.

Bonnefoy's own example is impressive. But there is, as he himself observes, a danger: 's'il y a dans les mots que nous employons cette virtualité de présence, ce grand espoir,—il en découlera qu'on parlera sous ce signe, comme enivré, sans avoir critiqué, comme il se doit, notre pratique des choses.' [If we are to assume that the words we use contain this potential *presence*, this great hope—the result will be that we shall speak under this sign, as if intoxicated, without criticizing our practice of things as we should.] Thus, French poetry runs, according to Bonnefoy, a risk of emptiness and abstraction.

What Bonnefoy says of the ideal French poetic language is true at least to this extent: he has accurately summed up the type of language he himself uses. Poets' views on poetry are always views about their own particular style of poetry. But is he right about the differences between English and French? If he is, then the translator's task, faced with his work and the work of other like-minded poets, is likely to be a thankless one. These poems, done into English, will not become less abstract, only less convincing. I doubt if the English language believes in essences—it believes only in palpable objects, and essences are a matter of *suggestion*.

But is Bonnefoy's theory of the French language right in general? Is French really incapable of seeing the universe, not in a grain of sand (it can do that), but in any *particular* grain of sand? Or are Bonnefoy's attitudes due to his belonging to the Mallarmé tradition, those who feel that the real world of mud and lilies is unpoetic? If he is right, then the English reader runs the risk of unbalanced judgments on French poetry, which we cannot but see through English-tinted spectacles. And indeed this is what Bonnefoy suggests when he notes that the English are passionately fond of Laforgue and Corbière, who to the French are minor poets.

Well, one should perhaps remember the disastrous statements of those successive generations of French poets who have lauded the comic gaucheries of Edgar Allan Poe to the skies: one should perhaps reserve judgment. But, in the first place, is the mud and lilies argument not precisely what the modern movement in the arts has always been about? The revolution in poetry which the Romantics began, and which Baudelaire and Rimbaud brought to fulfilment, was largely (as such revolutions always must be) a revolution in *language*. Rimbaud and Apollinaire admitted into their poetry words hitherto impermissible—modernisms, slang, even obscenities. For the *word* is the *experience*, in poetry. Are whole areas of experience to be out of bounds to the French poet? And would Bonnefoy's views, if universally adopted, not even tend to move French poetry back to a kind of neo-classical phase?

I am therefore content that many younger poets than Bonnefoy are following other examples.[4] Not so much that of Francis Ponge, though he is certainly interested in grains of sand. He attempts to explore the thingness of things with what purports to be 'scientifically' exact method: he will spend three pages getting inside the skin of an apricot, or twenty or so describing 'the prawn in all its states'. His apparent use of scientific terminology is of course misleading, for his purpose is not scientific: such terminology is there to give the *impression* of scientific 'fact'. He is in reality France's most distinguished poet of the sense-data. He writes to make us taste, touch and smell in imagination, and to create, in poetry, an equivalent for the mysterious solidity of objects other than ourselves. Certainly this is a use of language which does not turn objects directly into essences, and which suggests the essences behind objects. But only a limited essence: sensations with *their* mystery, but not any further mystery.

The example of André Frénaud has, I suspect, been more instructive to the generation of 1930 (the decade after Bonnefoy). Frénaud's work gives a rather uneven impression, but this is partly due to the great variety of tones and styles he uses. Now Bonnefoy's argument, summarized above, relates in large measure to style and levels of discourse. In French there has traditionally been a much larger gulf between the spoken and the written word than in English, where we may fairly say that *Basic English* is common to both modes of discourse. But in French, even the word order may often be different.[5] Raymond Queneau mentions an interview with a distinguished writer where it was pretended that the interview had finished; the writer immediately 'took off his mask, his "orator's" mask, and began to talk quite another language.'

Now clearly this makes for variety: at the eloquent literary end of the scale we have Saint-John Perse, at the other the idiomatic jokiness of Queneau himself. French supports 'rhetoric' more easily than English. It is still very visibly an element in someone so completely contemporary as Jean Paul Guibbert. Take, for instance, the balanced splendour of the rhythm, the dignity of the language, the careful placing of the apostrophe in the first line of *Pour Béa IX*:

Tu avais, ô unique martyre en ce jardin,
Les yeux martyrisés . . .
[You had, O single martyr in that garden,
Martyred eyes . . .]

The literary norm is so different, in fact, from colloquial French that literary discourse finds the latter hard to assimilate. And I suspect this may be why 'rhetoric' has, in French, found it easier to survive. For literature needs a wide range of styles and tones, and if colloquial speech becomes taboo, 'normal' tone may be attributed to the literary language, and writers may feel that an *ultra*-literary style is needed to preserve the serious effect of the highest poetry.

The reaction, of course, against loftiness and dignity may then be all the fiercer. French poetry consequently has a flourishing colloquial tradition, exemplified here by Queneau, Duprey and Tardieu, and descending from Jarry, Apollinaire and the Surrealists. Some of this is mere literary snook-cocking, of exactly the kind one finds in Picabia's well-known picture of the 1920s, that showed a toy monkey nailed to a canvas, and bore around its frame the words '*Renoir, Rembrandt, Cézanne—Natures mortes*'.[6] But even at its slightest this has its own value, that of questioning our attitudes, or of taking an axe to the pompous clichés of 'literature'. In Queneau's *Art poétique*, for instance, the classic problem of inspiration is seen as a joke. There is a whole aesthetic, or rather anti-aesthetic, behind such a poem. It is that of the *Collège de 'Pataphysique*[7] to which not only Jarry and Queneau, but Boris Vian and Ionesco belonged: an aesthetic of the absurd: the trivial and the downright silly are parts of life and, if poetry records life, parts of poetry. But the clown's mask is a mask of tragedy and terror as well. Hence the disturbing overtones of Queneau's 'Un poème est bien peu de chose . . .', or Tardieu's '*Conseils donnés par une sorcière*'.

But to return; it may be that in French the range of styles between, say, the eloquence of Saint-John Perse and the raciness of Queneau, is of such breadth that it is excessively difficult to bridge. The writer's problem is to preserve the power and import of serious discourse whilst not abandoning the concrete reference of ordinary speech. André Frénaud's language can be seen as one attempt to bridge this gulf through an amalgam of different tones all accommodated to a single personal voice, the serious and the down-to-earth, the momentous and the momentary. In *Epitaphe* for instance, we find him deliberately choosing a word that Bonnefov, as we saw above, shuns: namely '*ricaner*' (to snigger):

'il ne me ricanera pas à la gueule'
[he won't snigger in my face]

For the overtones of the situation demand a note of contempt: and the situation itself thereby becomes more definite. The sense-data are given their due, and when Frénaud manages to accommodate their demands to those of serious poetry, his work points, I feel, to a possible solution.

Certainly the sense-data have returned in the work of several poets first published in the 1960s. Jacques Réda and Jean Pérol, for instance, habitually catch the bird of poetry by spreading first a net of details which, if not so almost palpably concrete as the details of a Hopkins or a Hughes, at least clearly evoke the outer world of the senses. *Matin d'octobre* and *Yorou* are very different poems of course, but both function in part through the attention they direct to details, which are found by the end of the poem to cast on the walls of the mind a pattern of an unexpected sort. And possibly a poetic experience gains additional depth if its surface is present too.

Nor do these poets seem to accept any *a priori* limits on the kind of vocabulary permissible to poetry. The extreme case here is no doubt Robert Marteau, whose language has often a concrete particularity which can easily be paralleled in English. Consider for instance the first section of *Travaux pour un bûcher* given here. But for range of vocabulary, no poet now practising in France can compare with Michel Deguy. His poetry is usually firmly based upon the sense-data: the starting-point of 'Moraine bleue . . .' is a particular impression. As he himself says,[8] 'Longtemps j'ai cru que certaines choses dans leur agencement, disons certains lieux, faisaient parabole. Non pas "à première vue", ni pour une description; mais dans leur rapprochement que le poème opère . . .' [I have long believed that in the way they are arranged, certain things, certain places for instance, constitute parables. Not 'at first sight', nor for descriptive purposes; but in the way the poem works a sort of *rapprochement* between them . . .] In other words, the poem creates an awareness of otherwise unstatable universals hidden in ordinary experiences, ordinary places; and Deguy normally 'begins with a flea and ends in God', as Bonnefoy says of English poetry. He considers everything to be grist to his poetic mill; and his technique involves the use also of the most abstract and technical of terms, and the most 'farfetched' of comparisons.

Some contemporary French poets are thus in healthy reaction against the attitudes of Bonnefoy. One might generalize and say that the Surrealists had tended to write a psychological poetry, that depicted (theoretically) unconscious states of mind. (Ironically, the poetry of the Surrealists reads more concretely than that, say, of Laude or du Bouchet.) Bonnefoy brought back the conscious mind, the intellect, but his poetry is still psychological. The new school has readmitted the sense-data, whilst continuing to write under the intellect's control.

There is little urban atmosphere in the poems I have chosen. This is partly no doubt a result of my own predilections: not that I regret or reject urban poetry—far from it—but what recent French examples of it I have seen appear to me ephemeral. France is still a country of great open spaces, containing a wide variety of countrysides of striking beauty; and the French poet's heart at the moment seems to be there rather than in Paris. It used to be said that French writers took the first train they could to the capital. But some exceptions to this rule have been seen recently: René Char lives in his beloved Provence; Jean Pérol tells me he detests Paris.

Nor do the poems here have much moralizing tendency. There is nothing Audenesque about them, nor do they even engage in the kind of meditation exemplified by Larkin's *Church-going*. It may be that Surrealism is to some degree responsible for this situation, for its poets spent most of their time writing a poetry that contained either no morality or the reverse of one. 'Épater le bourgeois' was their favourite game. From this extreme, some of them (for instance, Eluard and Aragon) fled to its opposite, and engaged in whole-heartedly political poetry. And for the French poet there seems no middle way between introspection and politics. France is in many ways a deeply divided country, scarred by the Occupation and its aftermath, its classes and power groups bitterly suspicious of each other. The French therefore do not appeal, as Larkin does, to a common-sense moral point of view supposed to be held by the ordinary man, a modest sort of decency, with overtones even of philistinism, and certainly a horror of decisive action. The French would feel this kind of attitude to be both unrealistic and—worse still—unintellectual. Moral judgments in French poetry are thus neither broadly humanist nor pragmatic nor tentative: they are pronounced by committed Catholics and Communists, and, outside France in the French-speaking world at large, by nationalists or the apostles of *négritude*.

Unfortunately most of this poetry strikes me as self-indulgent. Henri Pichette for instance writes:

Peuple de 89
Peuple de la Commune
Peuple de la Révolution d'octobre
Peuple debout après la Longue Marche . . .
[People of 1789
People of the Commune

People of the October Revolution
People still standing after the Long March . . .]

The final comment on this kind of thing was made by Yeats
when he observed that it is out of our quarrel with ourselves
that poetry is written, whereas our quarrel with others pro-
duces merely 'rhetoric'. (Here too, by the way, it is amazing
how often the political poets employ the language of arche-
types. Eluard's last poems are still full of sky, sea, stones and
sun, and poets such as Jean Marcenac follow his example.)

It has been said that such poets as Holub and Voznesensky
'explore the individual's public dilemma'. This of course is a
different matter again; and Yeats himself was deeply and
successfully involved in such exploration. But there are, I feel,
few convincing attempts to do this in France since the Occupa-
tion. The poets here tend to turn inward towards their private
worlds or to appeal to 'eternal values', expressed again in
terms of Nature. Thus, Henri Pichette's Poet 'assume une
ambassade à la faveur de courbes d'onde, de flèches d'arbres,
de plans d'azur coupés de lignes de crête, de villes à volonté le
long de méridiens fleuris . . .' [heads a deputation by favour
of wave curves, tree arrows, planes of blue intersected by
crests, towns ad lib along flowering meridians . . .][9] Or else
they stand as it were on the verge of great open spaces, finding
no 'sermons in stones', but rather an ever-fascinating enigma.
If English poetry at this moment is private, idealistic and un-
intellectual, then French poetry is private, idealistic and in-
tellectual. Perhaps—and despite May 1968— public dilemmas
are more agonizing in the Communist East of Europe—as
also no doubt in America?

The West Indies and Africa are a different story, of course.
But deeply felt causes do not automatically produce deeply
effective poetry, and since the advent of Aimé Césaire none
but the highest standards can henceforth be acceptable for
coloured poetry in French. In Canada too, where there are
also serious public dilemmas, and where poetry has now come
of age, the best work seems to me still to be inward-looking.
I have included two coloured and two French Canadian
poets, but practically none of their poems given here could be
said to involve a possible political theme.

Despite these generalizations, however, there is a consider-
able variety and richness in the present French poetic scene—

a variety which I suspect to be greater than that of contemporary Britain, and which illustrates the Continental tendency towards using the full gamut of linguistic possibilities open to the modern writer. These poets range from eloquence (Bonnefoy, Guibbert, Ouellette) to colloquiality (Queneau, Tardieu); from Surrealist black humour (Duprey) and dazzling imagery (Césaire) to an equally dazzling verbal experimentation of the most conscious and intelligent kind (Deguy); from traditional antipoetry (Queneau and Tardieu again) to the new antipoetic stance of Denis Roche; from wide-eyed delicacy (Guillevic) to constricted intensity (Jude Stéfan); from poetry of the most abstract absence (but most immediate human need—Jean-Claude Renard) to that of the more concrete and central tradition of modernism (Frénaud, Réda, Pérol, Marteau, Roubaud).

The reader will find no 'Concrete Poetry' here, though this international movement is as well represented in France as elsewhere. My motive for excluding it is that Concrete Poets are, in general, uninterested in Meaning,[10] which I take to be as inalienable an element of language as consciousness is of humanity. Similar considerations have led me to omit the poets of *Tel Quel*, such as Marcelin Pleynet. According to Sollers, one of their ideologists, 'l'écriture . . . n' "exprime" rien, ne "signifie" rien . . . .' [writing . . . 'expresses' nothing, 'means' nothing. . . .], these words being placed between inverted commas as if meaning had no meaning. *Tel Quel's* pronouncements have an arcane and delphic quality, but unless I am misinterpreting their position, they seem to be ultimately denying a connexion between experience and literature.[11] But if this were so, why read? It is true that the operation of reading does not seem to be imposed upon one by even a careful scanning of Pleynet's texts.

As in all anthologies, then, this is a personal choice, in part dictated by my preferences and by the view I take of the nature of poetry, in part by such factors as space and (relative) translatability. For translators are always betrayers, as everyone knows, but sometimes it becomes well-nigh impossible even to betray. None the less, some of my imprecisions are deliberate, as when 'lily of the valley' becomes simple 'lily', where a general term has been made a little more particular, or where in Deguy's *Phases* the poet's catalogue of 'figures of speech' has been reshuffled for rhythmic reasons.

I should like to thank those poets with whom I have discussed these texts, for their invaluable and patient assistance and advice; and to apologize to those I have not met for any involuntary distortion of their intentions that I may have committed. I am also most grateful to M. Jean-Michel Alamagny for the time he has spent discussing various fine points of translation with me.

NOTES

1. See my note on Garelli, p. 200.
2. *Un Rêve fait à Mantoue*, pp. 110–11.
3. It is perhaps worth speculating whether this assimilation of concrete, but general, French words to abstract entities is not assisted by the use of the definite article in French. 'Le' or 'la' is not only prefixed to 'stone', or 'eagle', but also to 'honour', 'peace', etc. And at least it is clear that in Bonnefoy, Torreilles, and other poets like them, the article is given almost abstractizing force.
4. I hope I shall not be taken to be attacking Bonnefoy. He is undoubtedly a major poet. I simply feel that if his doctrine were taken neat and became the universal beverage it would have a disastrously limiting effect. The point is simply that there is not just *one* way of writing poetry. And, to illustrate the virtues of Bonnefoy's type of approach to language, one could equally instance the work of Dupin. His *Grand vent* (p. 116), for example, presents a beautifully lonely image of Man's situation. The wind itself is the *pneuma*, the breath of life, which also will blow us all away. We live 'on heights' where this wind is more sharply felt. We have conquered nature, but our path is towards darkness. We are subject, like the corn our sustenance, to cyclical death and rebirth (e.g. the burning of the stubble and the entry of the flame into our bones). Wine and bread are human communion, our answer (both sufficient and insufficient) to the volcano's age, the vast temporal spaces of nature. 'Flesh will endure . . .': we foresee our end, as the wolf our onetime competitor did not, but flesh is obliged to endure this end in courage and hope before we return to the 'sea' from which (ultimately) we came. The suggestiveness of these elemental images is immeasurable: there is a whole subject for meditation in the image of 'the blows/That make us visible' for instance: these blows are the subatomic particles striking us, literally making us visible, literally battering at us, ripening us, ageing us, their speed serving as a measure of time (see Einstein), time that is implicit in 'ripening' and in the basalt, the igneous rock cast up from the age-old volcano. Dupin has here achieved imagery of such simplicity it is at first sight bewildering, but ultimately it unfolds wonderfully in the mind. The capacity of

French to achieve this kind of effect is clearly one of its especial strengths as a language.

5. Queneau gives as an example the literary (or 'correct') *Le gendarme a-t-il rattrapé son voleur?* 'translated' into colloquial French as *Il l'a-t-il attrapé, le gendarme le voleur?* where the words which give *grammatical* information are separated almost completely from those which provide *meanings*. (Queneau, 'Ecrit en 1955', *Bâtons, chiffres et lettres*, Gallimard.)

6. 'Still lives.' Or should one translate: 'Dead ducks'?

7. The Physics of Shock. But 'Pataphysics' has certainly the right overtones, with its reminiscence of 'Patacake, patacake . . .'

8. *Figurations*, Gallimard, 1969, p. 99.

9. In his dramatic poem *Les Epiphanies*, where he is lyrical, rumbustious and Rimbaldian. His later poetry however is stridently political, and, unfortunately, his best early (and non-political) work is very lengthy, and I have regretfully not included him.

10. There are occasional exceptions, of course. In Britain, Edwin Morgan is one.

11. Or at least between experience and the particular brand of 'writing' that they practise and advocate. Denis Roche, however, although he shares many of their views, is perhaps a slightly different case, and I have included him.

Poems

JEAN FOLLAIN
Glace rouge

L'AN MIL huit cent douze en Russie
quand les soldats faisaient retraite
au milieu de cadavres
d'hommes et de chevaux
avait gelé le vin robuste
la hache du sapeur
dut alors partager
entre tous même moribonds
le bloc de glace rouge
à forme de futaille
qu'aucun musée
n'eût pu jamais garder.

Les siècles

REGARDANT LA marque du sabot
de son cheval de sang
le cavalier dans cette empreinte contournée
où déjà des insectes préparaient leur ouvroir
devina la future imprimerie
puis pour lui demander sa route
il s'approcha du charpentier
qui près d'une rose
en repos contemplait la vallée
et ne lirait jamais de livres.

Dans le temps

AU TEMPS des innombrables suites
du roi Soleil
il avait gelé
une nuit sur la terre
l'homme après boire
avait essuyé sa moustache blonde
et la femme un peu regardé
les cristaux du givre
les siècles futurs attendaient
longue armée
au sommet des monts.

Red Ice

IN EIGHTEEN-TWELVE in Russia
when the soldiers were retreating
amid corpses
of horses and men
the lusty wine had frozen
the sapper's axe
had then to share
for all even the dying
the block of red ice
cask-shaped
that no museum
could ever have preserved.

The Centuries

LOOKING AT a hoofmark
left by his thoroughbred
the horseman in the curving print
where insects were already at their needlework
divined the future printing-press
then to ask his way
went up to a carpenter
resting by a rose
looking out across the valley
and who would never read a book.

Long Ago

AT THE time of the Sun King's
endless retinues
it had frozen
one night on earth
the man after drinking
had wiped his blond moustache
and the woman gazed a little
at the crystals of frost
future centuries were waiting
a long army
encamped along the mountaintops.

Chien aux écoliers

LES ÉCOLIERS par jeu brisent la glace
dans un sentier
près du chemin de fer
on les a lourdement habillés
d'anciens lainages sombres
et ceinturés de cuirs fourbus
le chien qui les suit
n'a plus d'écuelle où manger tard
il est vieux
car il a leur âge.

Toujours

L'ENSEIGNE s'érige
au-dessus d'une porte
où le chien vient gratter
l'homme dort.
Il a dit ramenant l'herbe
je préfère ma demeure
à tout au monde
mes fleurs rouges à mes filles.
Il ignore qu'un cristal
se multiplie.
N'empêche que sonne l'heure
comme à sa jeunesse altérée.
Si la maison croulait, auprès des ruines
un bouvreuil chanterait encore.

Le pacte

LES LUMIÈRES soufflées
les tenailles posées sur l'établi
le temps passe.
Résistent aussi l'aire en terre battue
les chaumes.
Ecrit à l'encre bourbeuse
frappé de cire noire
le pacte conclu entre puissances
demeure lourd de menaces.
L'enfant pauvre joue avec la boue   *over*

Schoolboys' Dog

THE SCHOOLBOYS play at breaking ice
on a path
near the railway
they're thickly clad
in old dark woollens
and worn leather belts
the dog that follows them
no longer has a bowl for supper
he's old
for he's their age.

Always

THE SIGN hangs
over a door
where the dog comes scratching
the man's asleep.
He said as he brought home the hay
I prefer my house
to anything in the world
my red flowers to my daughters.
He doesn't know that crystals
grow.
But still the clock strikes
as in his distant youth.
If the house collapsed, near the ruins
a bullfinch would still sing.

The Pact

THE LAMPS blown out
the pincers laid on the bench
time passes.
Survival too of fields of stubble
threshing-floor of beaten earth.
Written in muddy ink
sealed with black wax
the pact concluded between powers
hangs heavy with menace.
The poor child plays with mud

le riche avec le sable.
Une tristesse se répand
dans des salles sans écho.

Un crépuscule

LA PRESSE à bras ne sert plus
que tachent des encres durcies
les chambres à gaz s'éteignent
l'ombre d'une main effilée
se montrera précise
sur un mur sanglant
des fronts se rejoindront
les oiseaux se tairont
et par le sentier
des enfants porteront pour leur dîner
une écuellée
de haricots blancs dans leur sauce figés.

Allumez donc

LES OEILLETS du corset
jettent leurs reflets
des persiennes fermées
protègent un monde
dont l'illusion
s'effondrera.
L'heure a le goût de son temps.
Allumez donc les lampes
entend-t-on, voyons
c'est la nuit.

La barricade

SEUL IL n'arrête pas de revoir
malgré les arbres verts
comme dessinée à l'encre de Chine
la barricade;
l'air fouette les visages aigris
près d'une cage à vieux oiseaux
ceux qui têtus sourient
à l'amour exigeant
écoutent sonner l'heure.

over

the rich with sand.
Sadness spreads
in echoless rooms.

A Twilight

THE ARM-SCREW is out of use
spattered with hardened ink
the gas-chambers are turned off
the shadow of a tapering hand
will show up clear
on a bloody wall
foreheads will join again
birds will fall silent
and along the lane
children will carry for dinner
a bowlful
of broad beans congealed in their sauce.

Light Up Then

THE EYELETS of a corset
gleam
closed shutters
protect a world
whose illusion
will crumble.
The hour tastes of its time.
Light the lamps then
they say, after all
it's night.

The Barricade

ALONE HE can't stop seeing
despite the green trees
as if drawn in Chinese ink
the barricade;
the air whips soured faces
by a cageful of old birds
those who stubbornly smile
at love's demands
hear the hour strike.

L'homme a senti
au café du matin
sa doublure usée
à l'endroit du coeur.

JEAN TARDIEU
Fenêtre

UN PEU d'eau compense
l'excès de ce monde:
vide entre des pierres
elle feint l'absence
pour nous délivrer.

Fenêtre de l'air
surface effacée
n'ayant rien pour elle
la voici profonde
pour une pensée.

Vienne la tempête
la glace est ridée
tout l'esprit retombe
dans l'opacité!

J'étouffe je passe
je cherche en frappant
sur le sol épais
j'écoute j'attends

que le vent qui souffle
gagne assez de force
pour ouvrir l'espace
entre les objets.

Conseils donnés par une sorcière
(à voix basse, avec un air épouvanté, à l'oreille du lecteur)

RETENEZ-VOUS de rire
dans le petit matin!

N'écoutez pas les arbres
qui gardent les chemins!

over

At morning coffee
he felt
the threadbare lining
over his heart.

Window

A LITTLE water compensates
a surfeit of world:
empty between stones
it delivers us
by pretending absence.

Air's window
rubbed-out surface
possessing nothing
see how deep it is
for a thought.

If a storm comes
the glass is ruffled
the mind goes
opaque again.

I can't breathe
I move on I ask
knocking on solid earth
I listen and wait

for the wind to blow
such a gale
it'll open a space
between things.

Advice from a Witch
in a terrified whisper in the reader's ear

KEEP FROM laughing
at first light!

Don't listen to the trees
that watch over pathways!

Ne dites votre nom
à la terre endormie
qu'après minuit sonné !

A la neige, à la pluie
ne tendez pas la main !

N'ouvrez votre fenêtre
qu'aux petites planètes
que vous connaissez bien !

Confidence pour confidence :
vous qui venez me consulter,
méfiance, méfiance !
On ne sait pas ce qui peut arriver.

Le dilemme

J'AI VU des barreaux
je m'y suis heurté
c'était l'esprit pur.

J'ai vu des poireaux
je les ai mangés
c'était la nature.

Pas plus avancé !
Toujours des barreaux
toujours des poireaux !

Ah ! si je pouvais
laisser les poireaux
derrière les barreaux
la clé sous la porte
et partir ailleurs
parler d'autre chose !

Le milliardaire

JOHN APPORTAIT un plateau
sur lequel était un bateau.

Monsieur assis sur son lit
passa son habit et dit :

over

Don't tell your name
to the sleeping earth
till after the last stroke of midnight!

Don't hold out your hand
to snow and rain!

Don't open your window
except to small planets
whom you know well!

Trust for trust:
you who come to consult me,
beware, beware!
You never know what may happen.

Dilemma

I'VE SEEN prison cells
I've bumped into them
they were pure spirit.

I've seen celery
I've eaten it
it was plain matter.

No further forward!
Nothing but cells
nothing but celery!

Oh if I could only
leave the celery
inside the cell
the key under the door
and go off somewhere else
and talk about something else!

Millionaire

JEEVES BROUGHT a tray in
with a boat on it.

Milord sat on his bed
put on his suit and said:

'Posez ça là quelque part
je termine mon cigare.'

Une heure après John revint:
la fenêtre était ouverte
dans le lit il n'y avait rien
rien non plus sous la Plante Verte
et rien du tout sur le plateau.

—Monsieur est parti en bateau.

Procès-verbal

CET INDIVIDU était seul.
Il marchait comme un fou
il parlait aux pavés
souriait aux fenêtres
pleurait en dedans de lui-même
et sans répondre aux questions
il se heurtait aux gens, semblait ne pas les voir.

Nous l'avons arrêté.

Quand bien même . . .

QUAND BIEN même je verrais de mes yeux
les ancêtres peints sur les tableaux
descendre de leur cadre et marcher dans l'épaisseur
   du monde

Quand bien même je verrais de mes yeux
les routes de la terre se lever dans le ciel
gracieuses et penchées comme des jets d'eau

Quand bien même j'entendrais le soleil
(comment, lui ? oui le soleil le soleil)
me parler à voix basse m'appeler par mon nom

Quand bien même je prendrais tout à coup la stature
et le silence et la pesanteur d'une maison

Quand bien même j'aurais trouvé la clé
du grand tunnel qui traverse le globe
et je commencerais la lente glissade le long des parois   *over*

'Put it down somewhere
while I finish my cigar.'

Jeeves came back an hour later:
the window was open
nothing in the bed
nothing either under the Aspidistra
and nothing at all on the tray.

—Milord's sailed off in his boat.

Case for the Prosecution

THIS FELLOW was alone.
He was walking like a madman
talking to the pavement
smiling at the windows
weeping inside himself
answering no questions
bumping into people, seeming not to see them.

We arrested him.

Even if . . .

EVEN IF I saw with my own eyes
our painted ancestors
come down from their picture-frames and walk about
　　in the solid world

Even if I saw with my own eyes
the roads of the earth rise into the sky
slanting as gracefully as water-jets

Even if I heard the sun
(what, the sun? yes yes the sun)
whisper my name to me

Even if I suddenly grew to the size
and silence and weight of a house

Even if I found the key
to the great tunnel that runs through the earth
and began slowly sliding down its walls

Quand bien même je verrais de mes yeux
grouiller l'Autre Côté des choses

quand bien même quand bien même quand bien
  même . . .

—je croirais toujours à la sainte Réalité
qui partie de nos mains s'enfonce dans la nuit.

RAYMOND QUENEAU
Pour un art poétique

1. UN POÈME c'est bien peu de chose
à peine plus qu'un cyclone aux Antilles
qu'un typhon dans la mer de Chine
un tremblement de terre à Formose

Une inondation du Yang Tse Kiang
ça vous noie cent mille Chinois d'un seul coup
vlan
ça ne fait même pas le sujet d'un poème
Bien peu de chose

On s'amuse bien dans notre petit village
on va bâtir une nouvelle école
on va élire un nouveau maire et changer les jours de marché
on était au centre du monde on se trouve maintenant près
   du fleuve océan qui ronge l'horizon

Un poème c'est bien peu de chose

5. Bon dieu de bon dieu que j'ai envie d'écrire un petit poème
Tiens en voilà justement un qui passe
Petit petit petit
viens ici que je t'enfile
sur le fil du collier de mes autres poèmes
viens ici que je t'entube
dans le comprimé de mes oeuvres complètes
viens ici que je t'enpapouète
et que je t'enrime
et que je t'enrythme
et que je t'enlyre
et que je t'enpégase   *over*

Even if I saw with my own eyes
the teeming Other Side of things

even if even if even if . . .

—I should still believe in sacred Reality
that drops from our hands and sinks into the night.

For an Ars Poetica

1. A POEM's nothing much
hardly more than a cyclone in the West Indies
a typhoon in the China Sea
an earthquake in Formosa

One flooding of the Yang Tse Kiang
drowns off a hundred thousand Chinese at one go
bing
it doesn't even make the subject of a poem
Nothing much

We get along nicely in our little village
we're going to build a new school
we're going to choose a new mayor and change the market days
we used to be at the centre of the world now we're near
    river Ocean gnawing away the horizon

A poem's nothing much

5. Lord lord how I want to write a little poem
Goodness there's one just passing
Darling darling darling
come here so I can thread you
on the necklace of my other poems
come here so I can bottle you
in the pill of my collected works
come here so I can bardolize you
and rime you
and rhythm you
and lyric you
and high-horse you

et que je t'enverse
et que je t'enprose

la vache
il a foutu le camp

9. Ce soir
si j'écrivais un poème
pour la postérité ?

fichtre
la belle idée

je me sens sûr de moi
j'y vas
et

à
la
postérité
j'y dis merde et remerde
et reremerde

drôlement feintée
la postérité
qui attendait son poème

ah mais

ARMEN LUBIN
Sans rien autour

N'AYANT PLUS de maison ni logis,
Plus de chambre où me mettre,
Je me suis fabriqué une fenêtre
Sans rien autour.

Fenêtre encadrant la matière
Par le tracé tendre de son contour,
Elle s'ouvre comme la paupière,
Se ferme sans rien autour.

Se sont dépouillées les vieilles amours,
Mais la fenêtre dépourvue de glace

over

and verse you
and prose you

blast it
she's buggered off

9. This evening
what if I wrote a poem
for posterity?

christ
what a good idea

I'm feeling sure of myself
here goes
and

to
post
erity
I say shit and shittagen
and shittagen

caught you there
posterity
waiting for your poem

and how

Nothing Round It

WITHOUT A house or lodgings,
No room to sit in any more,
I've built myself a window
With nothing round it.

A window framing matter
With its soft outline.
It opens like an eyelid
And closes with nothing round it.

All the old loves have been stripped off,
But this window without panes

Gagne les hauteurs, elle se déplace,
Avec son cadre étonnant,

Qui n'est ni chair ni bois blanc,
Mais qui conserve la forme exacte
D'un oeil parcourant sans ciller
L'espace soumis, le temps rayé.

Et je reste suspendu au cadre qui file,
J'en suis la larme la plus inutile
Dans la nuit fermée, dans le petit jour,
Ils s'ouvrent à moi sans rien autour.

Dimanche

PLUS AUCUN couple pour la chambre de passe
Qui a le grand confort, des rideaux rouges, et par place
Des gravures où l'on voit de longues jambes,
Des bas blancs à jarretières bleues,
Des oreillers pansus sous des baldaquins.
Le dimanche est si beau que l'hôtel est délaissé,
L'hôtel des hôteliers et des deux cariatides.
Il n'y a plus qu'un grand silence liquide
Avec des serviettes d'une blancheur accentuée,
Avec des gouttelettes pures qui s'échappent,
Qui s'échappent toute nues d'un robinet.
Il n'y a plus qu'un grand silence liquide
Jusqu'au fond de la gravure où reste étendue
Une reine de beauté à demi nue
Que des hommes entourent, graves et artistes.
Ces hommes-là prennent le moulage du sein,
Tandis que par respect à la reine
Et à la dynastie régnante,
La garde suisse qui sera massacrée
Rengaine ses baïonnettes étincelantes.

Amour de Paris

L'ANNÉE DE mon premier, de mon grand amour
Ce fut l'année même des horloges lumineuses.
Ce fut cette année-là que dans nos carrefours
On les dressa avec un grand feu intérieur
Et Paris ne fut qu'une clarté radieuse,

over

Floats upwards, travels
In its puzzling frame

That is neither flesh nor whitewood
But keeps the exact shape
Of an eye, unblinking, surveying
Banded time, submissive space.

And I stay fastened to the moving frame,
I, its most unnecessary tear
At dead of night, at break of day,
They open to me with nothing round them.

Sunday

NO MORE couples for the streetwalker's room
With its highclass fittings, red curtains, prints here and there
Showing long legs,
White stockings with blue garters,
Big-bellied pillows under canopies.
It's such a fine Sunday the hotel's deserted,
Left to the hoteliers and two caryatids.
Nothing but a great liquid silence,
Startlingly white towels,
Clear droplets dripping,
Running naked from a tap.
Nothing but a great liquid silence
Lapping the frame of a print
Where a half-naked beauty-queen reclines
Amid a group of solemn, arty-looking men.
They take the measure of her bosom,
While out of respect for the queen
And the reigning dynasty,
The Swiss guard about to be massacred
Sheathe their glittering bayonets.

A Paris Love-Affair

THE YEAR of my first, my greatest love
Was the year of the luminous clocks.
It was the year they stood at every crossroad
With a big fire inside
And Paris was one radiant brightness,

Clarté qui m'était due.

Par la suite il a plu trois jours sur trois
Dans l'humide et l'obscur on marcha
On marcha, on marcha le long de la Seine
Mais s'il est des heures dont je me souviens
Ce sont celles qui furent gravées par le dedans
Avec du noir sur du blanc légendaire,
Avec du noir à ne pas dire.

Le passager clandestin

L'HÔPITAL ACCUEILLE les éclopés de la foire,
Ceux qui avaient misé dans les jeux à miroir.

Il les accueille comme on abat à bout portant,
Le mal physique a soumis même les dissidents.

Même l'enfance oubliée qui soudain se montre,
Même l'enfance qui soupèse le pour et le contre

Afin de savoir si les ténèbres seront comblées.
Vus d'en bas, ils semblent immenses nos démêlés.

Immense le plafond, immense la noire veilleuse
Drossée, engloutie par la marée houleuse,

Mais en bon matelot sachant lover une corde
La douleur touche son homme pour qu'il se torde.

Elle le met en boule, les genoux dans le menton,
Elle le met en boule, en boule sur le ponton,

Jusqu'à ce qu'il soit lové selon l'art du capitaine,
Avec trou dans le milieu pour un passager clandestin.

Minuit

LE VENT bouscule les plus gros déménageurs
Dont les meubles sortent en tumulte de la forêt.
A l'hôpital le silence s'étale plus qu'ailleurs
Quand l'homme se démeuble au dernier degré.

L'arrière-pays n'est plus pour l'homme,
Pour l'homme étalé. Il est la bête de surface
Descendu de ses hauteurs, remonté des profondeurs,
A l'hôpital il y a un mur plus qu'ailleurs.

over

A brightness I deserved.

Afterwards it rained three days out of three,
We walked in the wet dark
We walked, walked by the Seine
But if there are hours I remember
They are those incised within me
In black on legendary white,
In black beyond description.

The Stowaway

THE HOSPITAL welcomes the cripples of the fair,
Those who placed bets on looking-glass games.

Its welcome is a knockdown blow,
Illness lays even the rebellious low.

Even lost childhood suddenly reborn,
Even childhood weighing up the pros and cons

To know if darkness will be finalized.
From down here, our struggles seem immense.

Immense the ceiling, immense the black nightlight
Adrift, swallowed by the sea-swell.

But like a good sailor who can coil a rope
Pain handles its man to make him writhe.

It winds him in a ball, knees to chin,
It winds him in a ball on the lighter's deck,

Till he is coiled the captain's way,
With a hole in the middle for a stowaway.

Midnight

GUSTS OF wind jostle the removers
Whose furniture bursts from the forest fortissimo.
In hospital, silence spreads thicker than elsewhere
When Man's unfurnished to the last degree.

There's no back country for Man,
Supine Man. He's a creature of surfaces,
Dragged down from his heights, tugged up from his depths;
In hospital, walls are walls more than elsewhere.

Plus rien ne passe sinon l'attentat ultime
Qui colle les paupières pour qu'elles se suppriment,
Sinon la glace qui pose une bonne couche
Au-dessus du mal pour en cautériser la bouche.

Moi, je ne dis mot, pour garder l'espoir d'un accord.
Nous serions disposés à abandonner le corps
S'il n'était déjà si solitaire dans le drame,
Il fait toujours minuit lorsqu'on parle de l'âme.

JEAN-JOSEPH RABÉARIVELO

La PEAU de la vache noire est tendue,
tendue sans être mise à sécher,
tendue dans l'ombre septuple.

Mais qui a abattu la vache noire
morte sans avoir mugi, morte sans avoir beuglé,
morte sans avoir été poursuivie
sur cette prairie fleurie d'étoiles ?

La voici qui gît dans la moitié du ciel.

Tendue est la peau
sur la boîte de résonance du vent
que sculptent les esprits du sommeil.

Et le tambour est prêt
lorsque se couronnent de glaïeuls
les cornes du veau délivré
qui bondit
et broute les herbes des collines.

Il y résonnera,
et ses incantations deviendront rêves
jusqu'au moment où la vache noire ressuscitera,
blanche et rose,
devant un fleuve de lumière.

QUEL RAT invisible,
venu des murs de la nuit,
grignote le gâteau lacté de la lune ?
Demain matin,

Nothing can happen now but one last murderous assault
Gumming up the eyelids to force them to succumb,
Except ice laying down a good coating
Over pain, to cauterize the mouth.

I keep mum, and cling to hopes of compromise.
We'd be ready to forsake our bodies
If they weren't so alone on stage now;
When you mention the soul it's always midnight.

THE BLACK cow's hide is stretched,
stretched without putting out to dry,
stretched in sevenfold shadow.

But who slaughtered the black cow
dead without lowing, dead without bellowing,
dead without being pursued
on that meadow flowering with stars?

There she is, lying across half the sky.

Her hide is stretched
on the wind's sounding-box
carved by the spirits of sleep.

And the drum is ready
when they crown with sword-lilies
the horns of the calf delivered
bounding
grazing on the hills.

It will beat there,
and its incantations turn to dreams
till the moment when the black cow comes alive,
pink and white,
by a river of light.

WHAT INVISIBLE rat
scuttles from walls of night
to gnaw the milk-cake moon?
Tomorrow morning

quand il se sera enfui,
il y aura là des traces de dents sanglantes.

    Demain matin,
ceux qui se seront enivrés toute la nuit
et ceux qui sortiront du jeu,
en regardant la lune,
balbutieront ainsi:
'A qui est cette pièce de quat'sous
qui roule sur la table verte ?'
'Ah ! ajoutera l'un d'eux,
l'ami avait tout perdu
et s'est tué !'

Et tous ricaneront
et, titubant, tomberont.
La lune, elle, ne sera plus là:
Le rat l'aura emportée dans son trou.

ANDRÉ FRÉNAUD
Épitaphe

QUAND JE remettrai mon ardoise au néant
un de ces prochains jours,
il ne me ricanera pas à la gueule.
Mes chiffres ne sont pas faux,
ils font un zéro pur.
Viens mon fils, dira-t-il de ses dents froides,
dans le sein dont tu es digne.
Je m'étendrai dans sa douceur.

Maison à vendre

TANT DE gens ont vécu là qui aimaient
l'amour, le réveil et enlever la poussière.
Le puits est sans fond et sans lune,
les anciens sont partis et n'ont rien emporté.
Bouffe le lierre sous le soleil d'hier,
reste la suie, leur marc de café.
Je m'attelle aux rêves éraillés.
J'aime la crasse de l'âme des autres,
mêlée à ces franges de grenat,

over

he'll be gone
leaving marks of bloodstained teeth.

Tomorrow morning
all-night drunkards
and card-players leaving
will look at the moon
and stammer:
'Whose is that tanner
rolling on the green table?'
'Oh,' someone'll reply,
'our friend gambled everything away
and killed himself.'

And they'll all guffaw
and stagger and fall.
As for the moon, she won't be there:
the rat will have carried her off to his hole.

Epitaph

WHEN I present my slate to Nothingness
one day soon,
he won't snigger in my face.
My figures aren't fiddled,
they add up to absolute zero.
Come my son, he'll say with his cold teeth,
to the bosom you deserve.
I shall lie down in his gentleness.

House for Sale

SO MANY folk lived here who loved
love, waking up, and dusting.
The well is bottomless and moonless,
the old owners have left and taken nothing with them.
The ivy spreads under yesterday's sun,
leavings of soot, old coffee-grounds.
I harness myself to frayed dreams,
love the scourings of other people's souls,
mixed with those garnet fringes,

le suint des entreprises manquées.
Concierge . . . J'achète, j'achète la baraque.
Si elle m'empoisonne, je m'y flambe.
On ouvrira les fenêtres . . . Remets la plaque.
Un homme entre, il flaire, il recommence.

Les Rois Mages

AVANCERONS-NOUS aussi vite que l'étoile ?
La randonnée n'a-t-elle pas assez duré ?
Réussirons-nous enfin à l'égarer
cette lueur au milieu de la lune et des bêtes,
qui ne s'impatiente pas ?

La neige avait tissé les pays du retour
avec ses fleurs fondues où se perd la mémoire.
De nouveaux compagnons se mêlaient à la troupe,
qui sortaient des arbres comme les bûcherons.
Le Juif-errant peinait, aux blessures bafouées.
Des fourrures couvraient le roi noir malade à mourir.
Le pasteur de la faim est avec nous,
ses yeux bleus éclairent son manteau d'épluchures
et le troupeau rageur des enfants prisonniers.

Nous allions voir la joie, nous l'avons cru,
la joie du monde née dans une maison par ici.
C'était au commencement. Maintenant on ne parle pas.
Nous allions délivrer un tombeau radieux
marqué d'une croix par les torches dans la forêt.

Le pays n'est pas sûr, les châteaux
se glissent derrière nous.
Pas de feu dans l'âtre des relais. Les frontières
remuent à l'aube sous les coups défendus.
Nos paumes qui ont brisé les tempêtes de sable
sont trouées par le charançon et j'ai peur de la nuit.

Ceux qui nous attendaient dans le vent de la route
se sont lassés, le chœur se tourne contre nous.
Par les banlieues fermées à l'aube, les pays sans amour,
nous avançons mêlés à tous et séparés
sous les lourdes paupières de l'espérance.
La peur haletait comme une haridelle.   *over*

the ooze of ambitions gone awry.
Caretaker! I'll buy, I'll buy the place.
If it poisons me, I'll burn myself down.
Open the windows . . . Put up the name-plate.
Someone enters, sniffs the air, begins again.

The Magi

SHALL WE travel as fast as the star?
Hasn't the trip been long enough already?
Shall we succeed in losing at last
that glow between moon and beast,
taking its time?

The snow had embroidered the lands of returning
with its melted flowers where memory is lost.
New companions joined our band,
emerging from the trees like woodcutters.
The Wandering Jew toiled along, his injuries derided.
The black king was wrapped in furs and deadly sick.
The shepherd of hunger is among us,
his blue eyes illuminate his coat of parings
and the furious flock of captive children.

We were going to see joy, so we thought,
the world's joy born in a house hereabouts.
That was at the beginning. Now we don't speak.
We were going to deliver a radiant tomb
marked with a cross by forest torches.

It's a perilous land this, the castles
stealthy behind our backs.
No fires in the inn hearths. The frontiers
shift at dawn under forbidden strokes.
Our palms that broke sandstorms
are weevil-riddled and I fear the night.

Those who waited for us in the wind of the road
have grown tired, chorus their protests.
Through suburbs shuttered at dawn, loveless country,
we pass together and not together
beneath hope's heavy eyelids.
Terror panting like an old nag.

Nous arriverons trop tard, le massacre est commencé,
les innocents sont couchés dans l'herbe.
Et chaque jour nous remuons des flaques dans les contrées.
Et la rumeur se creuse, des morts non secourus
qui avaient espéré en notre diligence.

Tout l'encens a pourri dans les boîtes en ivoire
et l'or a caillé nos coeurs comme du lait.
La jeune fille s'est donnée aux soldats,
que nous gardions dans l'arche pour le rayonnement,
pour le sourire de sa face.

Nous sommes perdus. On nous a fait de faux rapports.
C'est depuis le début du voyage.
Il n'y avait pas de route, il n'y a pas de lumière.
Seul un épi d'or sorti du songe,
que le poids de nos chutes n'a pas su gonfler.
Et nous poursuivons en murmurant contre nous,
tous les trois brouillés autant qu'un seul
peut l'être avec lui-même.
Et le monde rêve à travers notre marche
dans l'herbe des bas-lieux.
Et ils espèrent quand nous nous sommes trompés de chemin.

Egarés dans les moires du temps, les durs méandres
qu'anime le sourire de l'Enfant,
chevaliers à la poursuite de la fuyante naissance
du futur qui nous guide comme un toucheur de bœufs,
je maudis l'aventure, je voudrais retourner
vers la maison et le platane
pour boire l'eau de mon puits que ne trouble pas la lune
et m'accomplir sur mes terrasses toujours égales
dans la fraîcheur immobile de mon ombre.

Mais je ne puis guérir d'un appel insensé.

Autoportrait

TRISTE ET gras, l'oeil gonflé par une perle opaque,
le verbe alourdi par les venaisons,
touffu comme une étoile louche,
tout fou comme un veau sous la lune court,
juste comme un tambour enterré non loin,   *over*

We'll arrive too late, the massacre has begun,
the innocents are lying in the grass.
And we splash up puddles every day in every land.
And the murmur gets hollower, of the dead unrescued
who trusted in our diligence.

The incense has gone rancid in its ivory boxes
and the gold has curdled our hearts like milk.
The girl has given herself to the soldiers,
whom we kept in the ark for her radiance,
the smile on her face.

We are lost. We've been given false directions.
From the very start of the journey.
There was no road, there is no light.
Only a golden cornspike out of a dream,
that the weight of our falling has not swollen.
And we go on, murmuring at ourselves,
on as bad terms as a man
can be with himself.
And the world dreams in our progress
through the grass of the bottom-lands.
And they hope when we have missed our way.

Straying in time's watered silk, the rough meanders
given life by the Child's smile,
knights in quest of the receding birth
of the future that prods us like an ox-herd,
I curse the whole venture, I want to return
to home and plane-tree
to drink the water of my well untroubled by the moon,
and fulfil myself on my terraces, always flat
in the still coolness of my own shadow.

But I cannot be free of this senseless call.

Self-portrait

PUDGY AND mournful,
an opaque pearl bulging his eye,
speech thickened by venison,
bushy as a cross-eyed star,
cracked as a calf running in the moonlight,
steady as a drum buried not far off,

qui bat s'arrête puis repart,
verdoyant comme une moisissure qui ronge son mur
et sourit alors,
sans égards pour le bonheur,
sans place enviable,
droitement dans sa démarche hostile,
gauchement roulant des yeux et des r
dans le charbon d'enfance et dans tous autres,
se niant lentement, s'élève
un homme porte-lumière.

Nourritures de la terre

DEUX YEUX coulés parmi les herbes
ne distraient pas le temps
d'aller à son allure
sans mauvaise intention
et le cœur du pendu,
qui s'est arrêté court
repartira tantôt
parmi les fleurs qui sont réjouissance,
puis s'éparpillent.

La femme de ma vie

MON ÉPOUSE, ma loyale étoffe,
ma salamandre, mon doux pépin,
mon hermine, mon gros gras jardin,
mes fesses, mes vesses, mes paroles,
mon chat où j'enfouis mes besoins,
ma gorge de bergeronnette.

Ma veuve, mon essaim d'helminthes,
mes boules de pain pour mes mains,
pour ma tripe sur tous mes chemins,
mon feu bleu où je cuis ma haine,
ma bouteille, mon cordial de nuit,
le torchon pour essuyer ma vie,
l'eau qui me lave sans se tacher.

Ma brune ou blanche, ma moitié,
nous n'aurions fait qu'une couleur,

over

beating stopping then starting again,
verdant as a mould that eats its wall
then smiles,
irreverent of happiness,
having no enviable place,
with straightforward prickly ways,
gauchely rolling his eyes and his r's,
in his childhood's coal and all others,
slowly negating himself, there stands
a human light-projector.

Foods of the Earth

TWO EYES drained into the grass
don't hinder time
from moving at its own pace
with no ill will
and the heart of the hanged man
stopped dead
but will soon beat again
among flowers that are jubilation,
then are scattered.

The Woman of My Life

MY WIFE, my loyal fabric,
my salamander, my sweet peach-stone,
my weasel, my big fat garden,
my parts, my farts, my parts of speech,
my pussy-earth for all my doings,
my wagtail breast.

My widow, my swarm of tapeworms,
my loaves of bread to handle,
to victual all my journeys,
my blue fire boiling up my hates,
my bottle, my bedtime drink,
the towel for rubbing my life down,
the water to wash me and stay sweet.

Brown-haired or white, my other half,
we would have made one colour,

un soleil-lune à tout casser,
à tous les deux par tous les temps,

si un jour je t'avais reconnue.

Si l'amour fut

MON AMOUR, était-ce toi ou mon seul élan,
le nom que ma parole a donné à son désir.
As-tu existé, toi l'autre ? Etait-il véritable,
sous de larges pommiers entre les pignons,
ce long corps étendu tant d'années ?

L'azur a-t-il été un vrai morceau du temps ?
N'ai-je pas imaginé une vacance dans l'opaque ?
Étais-tu venue, toi qui t'en es allée ?
Ai-je été ce feu qui s'aviva, disparut ?

Tout est si loin. L'absence brûle comme la glace.
Les ramures de mémoire ont charbonné.
Je suis arrêté pour jusqu'à la fin ici,
avec un souvenir qui n'a plus de figure.

Si c'est un rêve qu'éternel amour,
qu'importe j'y tiens.
J'y suis tenu ou je m'y trouve abandonné.
Désert irrémédiable et la creuse fierté.
Quand tu reviendras avec un autre visage,
je ne te reconnais pas, je ne sais plus voir, tout n'est rien.

Hier fut. Il était mêlé de bleu et frémissait,
ordonnancé par un regard qui change.
Une chevelure brillait, violemment dénouée,
recomposée autour de moi, je le croyais.
Le temps remuait parmi l'herbe souterraine.
Éclairés de colère et de rire, les jours battaient.
Hier fut.
Avant que tout ne s'ébranlât un amour a duré,
verbe qui fut vivant, humain amour mortel.

Mon amour qui tremblait par la nuit incertaine.
Mon amour cautionné dans l'œil de la tempête
et qui s'est renversé.

a sun-moon fit to raise the roof,
for both together, fit for all weather,

if only we had ever met.

If Love has Been

MY LOVE, was it you or my own impulse,
the name my speech gave its longing.
Did you exist, you the Other? Was it real,
under broad apple-trees among the gables,
your long body stretched across the years?

Was the blue sky a true slice of time?
Did I just imagine a rift in the opaque?
Did you arrive, you who went away?
Was I the fire that flared, went out?

It's all so distant. Absence sears like ice.
The branches of memory have charred.
I remain here halted till the end
with a memory that has no face.

If eternal love is just a dream,
so what, I hold to it tight.
I am held and helpless by it.
Irremediable desert and hollow pride.
When you return with another face,
I do not know you, my sight is gone, it's all nothing.

Yesterday has been. It was shot with blue and vibrated,
prescribed by a changing gaze.
Hair shone, violently undone,
reassembled around me, I thought.
Time stirred in the underground grass.
Lit with anger and laughter, the days flickered.
Yesterday has been.
Before it all tumbled, a love lasted,
word made flesh, mortal human love.

My love that trembled in the uncertain night.
My love that was guaranteed in the tempest's eye
and capsized.

Non pas un temple

LE TEMPLE enfermé dans la terre,
s'il est berceau il est tombeau.
La crypte parée dans la terre.
Venez amis, car il fait froid.

Pour s'entourer d'une lumière
il aurait fallu plus avant
creuser et dormir, à défaut
d'avoir su plaire au grand soleil.

Sans vos voix les murs ne s'éclairent,
frères, compagnons inconnus,
Descendez, célébrez la fête.
Et venez aussi, petits chiens.

Gardez-le si seul il est las.
Tous ses blasons et ses parures,
tous les objets bien trop aimés
ne font pas source ni lieu-saint.

La noce enfouie, le dieu sans foi.
Edifié hors du temps hagard,
le trésor pourtant s'obscurcit.
Toujours le désert prévaudra.
Demain déjà. Pourquoi la fête ?
Adieu amis, rien n'avait lui.

GUILLEVIC
Rond

—QU'EST—CE qu'il y a donc
De plus rond que la pomme ?

—Si lorsque tu dis : rond,
Vraiment c'est rond que tu veux dire,
Mais la boule à jouer
Est plus ronde que la pomme.

Mais si, quand tu dis : rond,
C'est plein que tu veux dire,
Plein de rondeur
Et rond de plénitude,

over

No Temple

THE TEMPLE locked within the earth,
if it is cradle it is grave.
The crypt decked out within the earth,
Come, friends, for it is cold.

To be encircled with a light
deeper you should have dug and slept,
unless you held the knowledge how
the great sun could be satisfied.

The walls do not light up without
your voices, comrades, unknown brothers.
Come down and celebrate the feast.
And come along too, little dogs.

Keep him if he alone is weary.
His coat-of-arms, his finery,
all objects only too well loved
provide no spring or holy place.

The buried revel, faithless god.
Erected outside haggard time,
the treasure nonetheless grows dark.
Always the desert shall prevail.
Tomorrow is already. Why
the feast? Goodbye friends, nothing gleamed.

Round

—WHATEVER CAN be rounder
than an apple?

—If when you say: round,
It's really round you mean,
Then a bouncing ball
Is rounder than an apple.

But if when you say: round,
It's full you mean,
Full of roundness
And round with fullness,

Alors il n'y a rien
De plus rond que la pomme.

Durée

COURTE EST la journée,
Courts sont tous les jours.

Courte encore est l'heure.

Mais l'instant s'allonge
Qui a profondeur.

Chanson

PAS PAR le plafond,
Pas par le plancher,
Petit enfant sage,
Tu ne partiras.

Pas brisant les murs
Ou les traversant,
Pas par la croisée,
Tu ne partiras.

Par la porte close,
Par la porte ouverte,
Petit enfant sage,
Tu ne partiras.

Ni brûlant le ciel,
Ni tâtant la route,
Ni moquant la lande,
Tu ne partiras.

Ce n'est qu'en passant,
A travers les jours,
C'est à travers toi
Que tu partiras.

Parabole

VENANT de loin

Avec toujours la même,
La régulière allure,

over

Then there is nothing
Rounder than an apple.

Duration

BRIEF IS the daytime,
Brief are the days.

Brief too the hour.

But the moment lengthens
That has depth.

Song

OUT THROUGH the ceiling,
Out through the floor,
Good little child,
You must not go.

Breaking or stepping
Through the wall,
Out through the window,
You must not go.

Out by the closed
Or the open door,
Good little child,
You must not go.

Skimming the sky,
Testing the road,
Mocking the heath,
You must not go.

Only in passing
Through day after day,
Through yourself
Will you go away.

Parabola

A LONG journey

At always the same
Steady pace.

Chaque pas que je fais
Est par avance inscrit,
Chaque lieu que je touche
Etait prédestiné
Mais par ma seule histoire.

Venant de loin

Vers cette volupté,
Mais si courte, au sommet.

Puis repartir
En sens inverse
Pareillement,
Exactement.

Point

JE NE suis que le fruit peut-être
De deux lignes qui se rencontrent.

Je n'ai rien.

On dit: partir du point,
Y arriver.

Je n'en sais rien.

Mais qui
M'effacera?

ANDRÉ PIEYRE DE MANDIARGUES
Le chasseur

LE PIRE c'est la neige
Dit Pierre encore
Et il voyait des biches
Courir dans l'œil de son chien,

Il voyait le cerf
Mourir encore
Au sein d'une blancheur salie,

La bête nue comme une fille
L'homme rouge
Les corps fumant dans l'air froid.

Each step I take
Is foreordained,
Each place I touch
Predestined
By my past alone.

A long journey

Towards this ecstasy,
So brief, at the summit.

Then off again
The opposite way
Identically,
Exactly.

Point

I AM only the fruit perhaps
Of two lines meeting.

I have nothing.

They say: to leave a point,
To reach it.

I can't tell.

But who
Can rub me out?

The Hunter

SNOW'S THE worst
Said Peter again
In the eye of his dog he could see
Does running,

He could see the deer
Dying again
Amid soiled whiteness,

The animal naked as a girl
The blood-red man
The bodies steaming in the cold air.

AIMÉ CÉSAIRE
Perdition

NOUS FRAPPERONS l'air neuf de nos têtes cuirassées
nous frapperons le soleil de nos paumes grandes ouvertes
nous frapperons le sol du pied nu de nos voix
les fleurs mâles dormiront aux criques des miroirs et
    l'armure même des trilobites
s'abaissera dans le demi-jour de toujours
sur des gorges tendres gonflées de mines de lait
et ne franchirons-nous pas le porche
le porche des perditions ?
un vigoureux chemin aux veineuses jaunissures
tiède
où bondissent les buffles des colères insoumises
court
avalant la bride des tornades mûres
aux balisiers sonnants des riches crépuscules

Soleil serpent

SOLEIL SERPENT œil fascinant mon œil
et la mer pouilleuse d'îles craquant aux doigts des roses
lance-flamme et mon corps intact de foudroyé
l'eau exhausse les carcasses de lumière perdues dans le
    couloir sans pompe
des tourbillons de glaçons auréolent le cœur fumant des
    corbeaux
nos coeurs
c'est la voix des foudres apprivoisées tournant sur leurs
    gonds de lézarde
transmission d'anolis au paysage de verres cassés
c'est les fleurs vampires montant à la relève des orchidées
élixir du feu central
feu juste feu manguier de nuit couvert d'abeilles
mon désir un hasard de tigres surpris aux soufres
mais l'éveil stanneux se dore des gisements enfantins
et mon corps de galet mangeant poisson mangeant
colombes et sommeils
le sucre du mot Brésil au fond du marécage.

Perdition

WE WILL strike the new air with our armoured heads
we will strike the sun with our wide open palms
we will strike the soil with our barefoot voices
the male flowers shall sleep in the creeks of mirrors and even
   the armour of trilobites
shall abase itself in the eternal halflight
on soft bosoms swelled with mines of milk
and shall we not enter the porch
the porch of perditions ?
a vigorous path to venous yellow stains
warm
where the buffaloes of untamed angers bound
runs
taking the bit of fullgrown tornadoes in its teeth
in the ringing cannas of rich twilights

Serpent Sun

SERPENT SUN eye mesmerizing mine
and the sea verminous with islands that crackle in the fingers
   of flame-thrower
roses and my unscathed lightning-struck body
the water uplifts the carcasses of light lost in the inglorious
   corridor
swirls of icicles halo the crows' charred hearts
our hearts
it is the voice of tame thunders turning on their crevice hinges
transmission of iguanas to the landscape of broken glasses
it is vampire flowers mounting to the relief of orchids
elixir of the central fire
righteous fire night-mango fire swarming with bees
my desire a hazard of tigers surprised in brimstone
but the tin-bright awakening is gilded with childhood strata
and my flint body eating fish eating
doves and slumbers
the sugar of the word Brazil at the bottom of the marsh.

La roue

LA ROUE est la plus belle découverte de l'homme et la seule
il y a le soleil qui tourne
il y a la terre qui tourne
il y a ton visage qui tourne sur l'essieu de ton cou quand
    tu pleures
mais vous minutes n'enroulerez-vous pas sur la bobine à
    vivre le sang lapé
l'art de souffrir aiguisé comme des moignons d'arbre par les
    couteaux de l'hiver
la biche saoule de ne pas boire
qui me pose sur la margelle inattendue ton
visage de goélette démâtée
ton visage
comme un village endormi au fond d'un lac
et qui renaît au jour de l'herbe et de l'année
germe

Statue de Lafcadio Hearn

SANS DOUTE est-il absurde de saluer cette poussée en plein océa
restée debout à la verticale parmi les griffures du vent
et dont le coeur à chaque battement déclenche
un délire vrai de lianes. Grande phrase de terre sensuelle
si bégayée aux mornes ! 'Et qui, qui veut' entendais-je
    hurler une voix sans dérision 'en boire
de l'Ame d'Homme ? De l'Esprit
de Combat ? De l'Essence par quoi qui tombe tombe pour
    se relever ? Du Meneur de Coeurs ? Du Briseur
de l'Enfer ?' Alors alors ma vue tarière força
et la vision pondit ses yeux sans rémission :

Yé grimpa au palmier
Nanie-Rosette mangeait sur un rocher
le diable volait autour
oint de graisse de serpent
d'huile des trépassés
un dieu dans la ville dansait à tête de boeuf

des rhums roux couraient de gosier en gosier
aux ajoupas l'anis se mêlait à l'orgeat   *over*

The Wheel

THE WHEEL is Man's finest and only discovery
there's the sun turning
there's the earth turning
there's your face turning on the axle of your neck when
    you cry
but you minutes won't you wind the lapped blood on the
    bobbin of life
the art of suffering sharpened like treestumps by winter's
    knives
the doe drunk with thirst
confronting me on the unexpected brim with your
face dismasted like a schooner
your face
like a village asleep at the bottom of a lake
and born again the day of grass and new year
seed

Statue of Lafcadio Hearn

NO DOUBT it's absurd to salute this growth in mid-ocean
standing up vertical against the clawing wind
whose heart at every beat releases
a frenzy of lianas. Great sentence of sensual earth
stammered to the mountains! 'And who, who will,' I heard
    a voice with no derision yelling, 'drink
of the Soul of Man? Of the Spirit
of Battle? Of that Essence by which the fallen fall to be
    raised again? Of the Leader of Hearts? Of the Harrier
of Hell?' Then then my auger sight strained hard
and vision laid its eyes unceasingly:

Yé climbed the palmtree
Nanie-Rosette was eating on a rock
round about flew the devil
anointed with serpent's fat
and dead men's oil
in the village danced a bullock-headed god

red rums sped from mouth to mouth
among the huts anis was blended with barley-syrup

aux carrefours s'accroupissaient aux dés et sur les doigts
   dépêchaient des rêves
des hommes couleur tabac
dans les ombres aux poches de longs rasoirs dormaient

des rhums roux couraient de gosier en gosier
mais aucun aucun qui formidable fît réponse
et sa muqueuse prêtât à la morsure des guêpes

O questionneur étrange
   je te tends ma cruche comparse
      le noir verbe mémorant
        Moi moi moi
car de toi je connus que ta patience fut faite
de la cabine de commandement d'un corsaire démâté
par l'orage et léché d'orchidées

Cadavre d'une frénésie

     L E S O U V E N I R d'une route
qui monte très fort dans l'ombrage des bambous
le vesou qui s'invente toujours neuf
et l'odeur des mombins

     on a laissé en bas
les petites jupes de la mer
les saisons de l'enfance
le parasol de coccolobes

je me tourne au virage je regarde par-dessus l'épaule
de mon passé c'est plein du bruit magique toujours sur le coup
incompréhensible et angoissant du fruit de l'arbre à pain
qui tombe et jusqu'au ravin où nul ne le retrouve
roule

la catastrophe s'est fait un trône trop haut perché
du délire de la ville détruite c'est ma vie incendiée
     Douleur perdras-tu
l'habitude qu'on hurle
j'ai rêvé face tordue
bouche amère j'ai rêvé de tous les vices de mon sang
et les fantômes rôdèrent à chacun de mes gestes
à l'échancrure du sort

     il n'importe c'est faiblesse   *over*

at the crossroads tobacco-coloured men
crouched over dice and hurried dreams up on their fingers
the shadows wore pockets where long razors slept

Red rums sped from mouth to mouth
but none none splendidly replied
and offered its mucus to the wasps' bite

O strange questioner
   I offer you my comradely jug
     black word of remembrance
       I i i
for from you I learnt that your patience was made
of the captain's cabin of a privateer dismasted
by the storm and licked by tongues of orchids

Corpse of a Frenzy

    MEMORY OF a road
climbing steeply through bamboo shade
cane-juice inventing itself afresh
and the scent of Spanish plums

    we've left below us
the little skirts of sea
the seasons of childhood
the parasol of seagrapes

I turn at the bend I look over the shoulder
of my past it's full of the magic sound at the time
tormenting and never understood of the fruit of the bread-tree
falling and into the gully where no-one can find it
dropping

disaster has built itself too high a throne
from the frenzy of the sacked town it's my life burned down
    Sorrow can you outgrow
the habit of shouting
I've dreamed my face contorted
my mouth rancid I've dreamed all the vices of my blood
and ghosts walked at my every gesture
at the keyhole of fate

    never mind that's weakness

veille mon coeur
prisonnier qui seul inexplicablement survit dans sa cellule
    à l'évidence du sort
féroce taciturne
tout au fond lampe allumée de sa blessure horrible

JEAN-PAUL DE DADELSEN
Bach en automne
II

J'AI CONNU jadis les jours de marche, les ormes vers le
    soir énumérés
        De borne à borne sous le soleil chromatique,
L'auberge à la nuit où fument quenelles de foie et cochon frais.
Jadis à libres journées j'ai marché jusqu'à Hambourg
    écouter le vieux maître.
        Haendel en chaise de poste s'en est allé
Distraire le roi de Hanovre; Scarlatti vagabonde dans les
    fêtes d'Espagne.
        Ils sont heureux.

Mais à quoi serviraient les pédales des orgues, sinon
        A signifier la route indispensable?
Sur ce chemin de bois, usé comme un escalier, chaque jour,
    que ce fût
Sous les trompettes de Pâques ou les hautbois jumeaux de Noël,
        Sous l'arc-en-ciel des voix d'anges et d'âmes,
De borne à borne répétant mon terrestre voyage, j'ai arpenté
        La progression fondamentale de la basse.

Au-dessus de la route horizontale par où les négociants
    partent non sans péril
        Marchander aux échoppes de Cracovie
Les perruques, les parfums, les peaux apportées des
    éventaires de Novgorod,
Seule l'alouette s'élance dans la verticale divine.
        Avant qu'à la suite de son Soleil
Hors de la tombe, de l'ordre, de la loi, l'âme éployée ne
    parvienne à jaillir,
        La terre apprise avec effort est nécessaire.

keep watch my heart
prisoner alone inexplicably outliving in its cell the evidence
    of fate
savage laconic
deep down lamp lit by its grim wound

Bach in Autumn
II

ONCE I knew days of walking, elms counted out towards
    evening
    From milestone to milestone under the chromatic sun,
The inn at night with its smoking pies of liver and fresh pork.
Once, dayfree, I walked right to Hamburg to hear the old
    master.
    Handel went off in a post-chaise
To entertain the King of Hanover; Scarlatti vagabonds it
    at Spanish fiestas.
        They're happy.

But what's the use of organ-pedals, except
    To point to the indispensable path?
On the wooden road, worn as a staircase, every day, whether
Under Easter trumpets or Christmas' twin oboes,
    Under the rainbow of souls' and angels' voices,
From milestone to milestone retracing my earthly journey,
    I've paced out
    The fundamental progression of the bass.

Above the horizontal road where businessmen set off, riskily
    enough
    To haggle in the markets of Cracow
For wigs, perfumes, skins brought from the stalls of
    Novgorod,
Only the lark soars divinely vertical.
    Before in pursuit of its Sun
Up out of grave and order and law the spread soul manages
    to fountain,
    The earth learned with effort is necessary.

Exercice pour le soir

ARRÊTE-TOI. Au lieu de haleter de seconde en seconde
Comme un torrent de roc en roc dévalant sans vertu,
Respire
Plus lentement et sans bouger, les pieds croisés, les mains jointes,
Regarde, comme si c'était le monde tout entier,
Un objet, menu et domestique, par exemple
Cette tasse.

Néglige sa courbure, ce bord ondulé, ces dessins bleus.
Ne considère que l'intérieur, cette cavité blanche, cette surface
Lisse.
L'eau n'est lisse ainsi que les soirs de grand calme
Après une journée qui rassemble et retient son bonheur
Au centre du silence où s'arrête son
Souffle.

Peux-tu nommer un jour, une heure, sans reflets d'hier,
Sans impatience de demain, où ton âme fut ainsi
Lisse ?
N'écoute pas ton cœur, ne compte pas ton pouls, ne songe pas
Au temps qui vers la mort te traverse, mais seulement
En arrêtant ton souffle regarde cette pure et seule qualité
De lisse.

Si maintenant tu apprenais à fixer ton regard, ta pensée,
Ton âme sans ciller sur quelques centimètres carrés de
Lisse,
Peut-être alors, sans fuir le monde, sans éviter les femmes,
Sans changer d'état, de pays, de nourriture,
Pourrais-tu espérer un jour commencer à comprendre
Le monde entier.

C'est une tasse sans valeur achetée dans une épicerie-mercerie
D'un village savoyard du côté de Boège et Séchemouille.
Elle n'est pas lisse.
Le microscope y trahirait un Himalaya d'aspérités.
Ce qui la fait lisse, c'est la lumière, ce sont tes doigts naïfs.
Pour un autre regard, peut-être, une tasse
Vaut une tête.   *over*

Exercise for Evening

STOP. INSTEAD of gasping on from second to second
Like a torrent tumbling futile from rock to rock,
Breathe
More slowly, motionless, feet crossed, hands clasped,
Gaze, as if at the whole world,
At one object, trivial and homely, for instance
This cup.

Ignore its curve, the wavy edge, the blue pattern.
Look only inside, at this white cavity, this smooth
Surface.
Water is not so smooth except on the stillest evenings
After a day that gathers and holds its contentment fast
In silence's centre where its breathing
Stops.

Can you name a day, an hour with no glimpses of yesterday,
No impatience for tomorrow, when your soul was as smooth
As this?
Don't listen to your heart, don't count your pulse, don't think
Of time passing through you towards death, but simply
Hold your breath, gaze at this pure and single quality
Of smoothness.

If you learnt now to fix your gaze, your mind,
Your soul without blinking on a few square inches of
Smoothness,
Perhaps then, without giving up the world, without avoiding
    women,
Without changing your job, your country, your food,
You might hope one day to begin to understand
Everything.

It's a cheap cup bought at a general store
In Savoy at a village near Boège and Séchemouille.
It isn't smooth.
A microscope would show a Himalaya of bumps.
What makes it smooth is the light, and your clumsy fingers.
Others might think a cup
Worth a head.

Autant que l'orgue solennelle ou la machine électronique,
Autant que l'orage équatorial et les courants du Pacifique
Cette tasse
Honore le Nom divin. Si demain tu étais exilé, tu n'aurais pas
Besoin, à condition de l'avoir regardée longtemps, à condition
De pouvoir dans ton cœur recomposer ce lisse, d'emporter
Ce tesson.

Voici l'entrée, non pas de la sagesse, ni du silence,
Ni du parfait pouvoir sur toi-même et ton ombre,
Mais d'une première
Cavité assez lisse pour contenir une poignée de paix.
Maintenant tu peux dormir, les pieds joints pour ne pas couper
Le courant, les mains jointes, maintenant tu peux
T'élever

Lentement, calmement un peu plus haut que ton corps étendu
Et dénoué, comme si tu n'habitais plus que ta tête
Ou tes narines
Ou les environs immédiats de l'œil pinéal;
Maintenant au-dessus de ton corps pacifié, au-dessus
De ta boîte à sornettes, dans le fluide lisse de ton âme éployée,
   tu peux
Veiller.

Dernière nuit de la pharmacienne

L E   V E N T par-dessus les glaciers accouru du désert
vient à peine fraîchi tourmenter les branches du grand sapin.
Quand tout est en travail, comment dormir, comment aussi
mourir ?

Sur les eaux lentes et lisses, les barques plates,
les barques noires sont, pareilles
à l'âme, presque indéfiniment amarrées.

L'année est longue avant de ramener
la fille distraite, le fils longtemps aimé de loin.
Les enfants qui riaient dans ses bras et sur ses seins
écrivent rarement à la femme du pharmacien,
même pour des remèdes.

La beauté est de peu de prix, sinon   *over*

As much as solemn organ or electronic instrument,
As much as equatorial gale or Pacific currents,
This cup
Honours the Divine Name. If you were exiled tomorrow—
provided
You'd gazed at it a long time, provided you could recreate
This smoothness in your heart—you wouldn't need to take
This shard.

Here is the door, not to wisdom or silence,
Or absolute mastery over yourself and your shadow,
But to a first
Hollowness smooth enough to hold a handful of peace.
Now you can sleep, feet touching so as not to break
The current, hands clasped, now you can
Rise

Slowly, calmly a little above your relaxed
Recumbent body, as if you dwelt now only in your head
Or your nostrils
Or beside the pineal eye;
Now above your pacified body, above
Your blether-box, in the smooth fluid of your outspread
soul, you can keep
Vigil.

Death of a Chemist's Wife

THE WIND over glaciers rushing from the desert
comes barely cooled to lash the tall fir's branches.
When everything's in travail, how to sleep, how above all
to die?

On the slow smooth waters, the flat boats,
the black boats are, just like
the soul, almost indefinitely moored.

The year is long in bringing back
her forgetful daughter, and son long loved from afar.
The children who laughed in her arms, at her breasts
seldom write to the chemist's wife,
even for medicine.

Beauty isn't worth much, except

comme un dernier appel qui ne sera plus entendu. O captive
parmi les saisons, le tonneau de choux frais
coupés dans la cave aux premiers givres d'octobre,
quand l'hirondelle soudain partie, on se réveille
dans le premier silence de l'arrière-saison.

Odile, la plaine est sans merci. La nuit
se plaignent les grenouilles en peine de se perpétuer.
La cigogne dans d'autres cheminées plonge son long bec lubrique.

Les pendules à gros sabots, le cœur à pas lourds
mesurent la nuit qui dérive à peine. Qu'il est dur
de rompre l'amarre ! Qu'il est long
le temps pour la traction de l'eau d'arracher
la chaîne qui depuis tant de temps retient à la berge !

Le cœur à gros sabots arpente les prairies nocturnes,
piétine sur la berge de l'eau
que très bientôt il faudra traverser.

ANNE HÉBERT
Vie de château

C'EST UN château d'ancêtres
Sans table ni feu
Ni poussière ni tapis.

L'enchantement pervers de ces lieux
Est tout dans ses miroirs polis.

La seule occupation possible ici
Consiste à se mirer jour et nuit.

Jette ton image aux fontaines dures
Ta plus dure image sans ombre ni couleur.

Vois, ces glaces sont profondes
Comme des armoires
Toujours quelque mort y habite sous le tain
Et couvre aussitôt ton reflet
Se colle à toi comme une algue

S'ajuste à toi, mince et nu,
Et simule l'amour en un lent frisson amer.

as a last appeal too late to be heard. O prisoner
among the seasons, the cask of fresh-cut cabbages
in the cellar at the first October frosts,
when the swallow has suddenly flown and you wake
in the after-season's first silence.

Odile, the plain is merciless. By night
the frogs complain at pains for self-perpetuation.
The stork thrusts its long salacious beak down other chimneys.

The heart slow-paced, the clocks in heavy clogs
measure the night out barely drifting. How hard it is
to snap the moorings! How long it is
for the tug of water to drag out
the chain fastened to the bank so long!

The heart in heavy clogs paces the meadows of night,
kicks its heels at the water's edge
that must be crossed so soon.

Stately Home

IT'S AN ancestral mansion
Without table or fire
Or dust or a carpet.

The perverse enchantment of this place
Resides in its polished mirrors.

The only activity possible here
Is being reflected night and day.

Into the hard pools fling
Your harder image without shadow or colour.

See, the mirrors are as roomy
As wardrobes
A dead man's sure to dwell behind the silvering
And instantly enwraps your reflection
Clings to you like seaweed

Fits round you, skinny and naked,
And simulates love in a slow sour throb.

Il y a certainement quelqu'un

IL Y A certainement quelqu'un
Qui m'a tuée
Puis s'en est allé
Sur la pointe des pieds
Sans rompre sa danse parfaite.

A oublié de me coucher
M'a laissée debout
Toute liée
Sur le chemin
Le cœur dans son coffret ancien
Les prunelles pareilles
A leur plus pure image d'eau

A oublié d'effacer la beauté du monde
Autour de moi
A oublié de fermer mes yeux avides
Et permis leur passion perdue.

Les grandes fontaines

N'ALLONS PAS en ces bois profonds
A cause des grandes fontaines
Qui dorment au fond.

N'éveillons pas les grandes fontaines
Un faux sommeil clôt leurs paupières salées
Aucun rêve n'y invente de floraisons
Sous-marines et blanches et rares.

Les jours alentour
Et les arbres longs et chantants
N'y plongent aucune image.

L'eau de ces bois sombres
Est si pure et si uniquement fluide
Et consacrée en cet écoulement de source
Vocation marine où je me mire.

O larmes à l'intérieur de moi
Au creux de cet espace grave
Où veillent les droits piliers

over

Someone Certainly

SOMEONE CERTAINLY has
Killed me
Then tiptoed away
Without interrupting his perfect dance.

Has forgotten to lay me flat
Has left me standing
Bound
On the road
My heart in its usual coffer
My eyes like
Their purest image of water

Has forgotten to rub out the world's beauty
Around me
Has forgotten to close my eager eyes
And permitted their hopeless passion.

The Big Fountains

BETTER NOT go to the woods
For deep inside them
Big fountains sleep.

Better not wake the fountains
Salt eyelids closed in mimic sleep
No dream invents exotic
White deepsea blossoms.

They don't reflect
The days around them
The lean and chanting trees.

The water in these dark woods
Is so pure, so purely liquid
And hallowed in this spring-flow
Sea-calling where I gaze.

O tears inside me
In the hollow of this solemn space
Where the upright pillars

De ma patience ancienne
Pour vous garder
Solitude éternelle solitude de l'eau.

Un bruit de soie

UN BRUIT de soie plus lisse que le vent
Passage de la lumière sur un paysage d'eau.

L'éclat de midi efface ta forme devant moi
Tu trembles et luis comme un miroir
Tu m'offres le soleil à boire
A même ton visage absent.

Trop de lumière empêche de voir;
            l'un et l'autre torche blanche,
                grand vide de midi
Se chercher à travers le feu et l'eau
                            fumée.

Les espèces du monde sont réduites à deux
Ni bêtes ni fleurs ni nuages.
Sous les cils une lueur de braise chante à tue-tête.

Nos bras étendus nous précèdent de deux pas
Serviteurs avides et étonnés
En cette dense forêt de la chaleur déployée.
Lente traversée.

Aveugle je reconnais sous mon ongle
            la pure colonne de ton cœur dressé
Sa douceur que j'invente pour dormir
Je l'imagine si juste que je défaille.

Mes mains écartent le jour comme un rideau
L'ombre d'un seul arbre étale la nuit à nos pieds
Et découvre cette calme immobile distance
Entre tes doigts de sable et mes paumes toutes fleuries.

Nos mains au jardin

NOUS AVONS eu cette idée
De planter nos mains au jardin

over

Of my one-time patience
Stand sentinel on
Solitude water's eternal solitude.

Silken Sound

SILKEN SOUND smoother than wind
Passage of light over landscape of water.

The glare of noonday fades your outline
You throb and glitter like a mirror
You give me the sun to drink
At your absent face.

Too much light blinds the eyes;
　　　　　both a white torch,
　　　　　　　　vast noon emptiness
To seek each other through fire and water
　　　　　　　　　　　smoke.

The world's species dwindle to two
No beasts or flowers or clouds.
A brazier under the eyelashes sings at full pitch.

Our arms are two paces ahead of us
Thunderstruck greedy retainers
In this dense forest of outstretched heat.
Slow crossing.

Blind I recognize under my nail
　　　　your heart's pure pillar standing
Its sweetness I invent to sleep with
And imagine so clearly I wince.

My hands open day like a curtain
A single tree's shadow unrolls night at our feet
And uncovers the calm still distance
Between your fingers of sand and my flower palms.

Our Hands in the Garden

WE HAD the idea
Of planting our hands in the garden

Branches des dix doigts
Petits arbres d'ossements
Chère plate-bande.

Tout le jour
Nous avons attendu l'oiseau roux
Et les feuilles fraîches
A nos ongles polis.

Nul oiseau
Nul printemps
Ne se sont pris au piège de nos mains coupées.

Pour une seule fleur
Une seule minuscule étoile de couleur
Un seul vol d'aile calme
Pour une seule note pure
Répétée trois fois.

Il faudra la saison prochaine
Et nos mains fondues comme l'eau.

Un mur à peine

UN MUR à peine
Un signe de mur
Posé en couronne
Autour de moi.

Je pourrais bouger
Sauter la haie de rosiers,
L'enlever comme une bague
Pressant mon cœur

Gagner l'univers
Qui fuit
Sans un cri.

Seule ma fidélité me lie.
O liens durs
Que j'ai noués
En je ne sais quelle nuit secrète
Avec la mort !

over

Ten-fingered branches
Little trees of bone
Dear flower-bed.

All day
We waited for the red bird
And fresh leaves
At our polished nails.

No bird
No spring
Were caught in the trap of our amputated hands.

For a single flower
A single minute star of colour
A single calm wing-beat
For a single pure note
Three times repeated.

We will have to wait for next season
And our hands melted like water.

A Wall Barely

A WALL barely
Symbol of a wall
Placed like a crown
Around me.

I could move
Jump the rose-hedge
Pull it off like a ring
Constricting my heart

Reach the universe
As it escapes
Without a cry.

Only my fidelity confines me.
Hard bonds
That I tied
In some secret night
With death!

Petit espace
Et mesure exacte
Des gestes futurs.

Au centre de l'enclos
La source du sang
Plantée droit
Cet arbre crispé
Et vous feuillages
Des veines
Et des membres soumis.

Par les jours calcaires et blancs,
Forme d'arbre en la durée
Bouleau clair
Aux sombres épanchements figés
Les doigts sans aucun désir
Etendus;
Mon cœur sera bu comme un fruit.

Couronne de félicité

LA MORT en louve morte changée
Cadavre pierreux à l'horizon brûlé

Le rêve petites fumées de village
Fument cent maisons dos à dos

Les dormeurs nagent dans une nuit sans étage
Fleurant l'algue et la mer

Ton visage lumière
Eveil
La vie d'un trait
L'amour d'un souffle

Le jour recommence
La nuit passe la ligne des eaux
L'aube toutes ailes déployées
Illumine la terre

La joie à bout de bras
Le poème au sommet de la tête hissé
Couronne de félicité

Small space
And precise measure
Of future movements.

At the centre of the enclosure
The blood-spring
Planted straight
A clenched tree
And you, foliage
Of veins
And obedient limbs.

By white limestone days,
Tree-shape in time
Pale birch
Its streams of dark sap frozen
Fingers with no desire
Spread out;
My heart will be drunk like a fruit.

Crown of Happiness

DEATH BECOME a dead she-wolf
Stone corpse on the scorched horizon

Dream, little smoke of a village
A hundred houses smoking back to back

Sleepers swim in a storeyless night
Smelling of sea and seaweed

Your face a light
An awakening
Life of a feature
Love of a breath

Day starts again
Night crosses the watershed
Dawn's outspread wings
Brighten the earth

Joy at arm's length
Poem hoisted head-high
Crown of happiness.

Les offensés

PAR ORDRE de famine les indigents furent alignés
Par ordre de colère les séditieux furent examinés
Par ordre de bonne conscience les maîtres furent jugés
Par ordre d'offense les humiliés furent questionnés
Par ordre de blessure les crucifiés furent considérés
En cette misère extrême les muets venaient en tête
Tout un peuple de muets se tenait sur les barricades
Leur désir de parole était si urgent
Que le Verbe vint à leur rencontre de par les rues
Le faix dont on le chargea fut si lourd
Que le cri «feu» lui éclata du cœur
En guise de parole.

ALAIN BOSQUET
Origine

A L'ORIGINE
il y aura trois cieux
le juste le moins juste et le frivole
à l'origine
il y aura
des soleils par douzaines
    comme des œufs dans les boutiques
    certains blancs certains noirs
    et certains habités par des vautours
à l'origine
il y aura
à chaque heure midi
à chaque heure minuit
    un équinoxe on veut dire une taupe
    et un printemps au milieu du printemps
    on veut dire une rose qui croasse
à l'origine
il y aura
un homme en cœur de cerisier
un homme en paroles de neige
un homme en naufrage de lune
à l'origine
il y aura
le divin gaspillage

The Offended

BY ORDER of famine were the needy lined up
By order of rage were the seditious examined
By order of clear conscience were the masters judged
By order of offence were the humbled questioned
By order of wounding were the crucified considered
At this pitch of distress the dumb led the van
A dumb populace massed on the barricades
Their desire for speech was so urgent
That the Word walked to meet them through the streets
The burden they loaded upon it so heavy
That the cry 'fire' exploded from its heart
Instead of speech.

Beginning

IN THE beginning
there shall be three heavens
the just the not-so-just and the flippant
in the beginning
there shall be
suns by the dozen
   like eggs in a shop
   some white some black
   and some containing vultures
in the beginning
there shall be
noon every hour
midnight every hour
   an equinox I mean a mole
   and a spring in the midst of spring
   I mean a rose that croaks
in the beginning
there shall be
a man with a cherry-tree heart
a man with words of snow
a man like the moon's shipwreck
in the beginning
there shall be
divine extravagance

From *100 notes pour une solitude*

TOUTE CONSCIENCE est mammifère, se dit-il.
Comme le vol très gars de la mouette,
sur toute chose
il met ses mots imprononçables.
Les eaux s'arrêteront.
Les orangers n'iront pas en exil.
Une patience
s'installera dans les métaux trop durs.
Il a quelque pouvoir:
on dirait une écume
poussant un petit crabe.

IL EST seul: on dirait un verbe défectif.
Des angles, des volutes,
des chiffres, des chimères
quelquefois le surpeuplent.
Comme de jeunes chiens,
il prend les mots sur ses genoux,
et les caresse.
Le mois de mai l'attend.
Il court parmi les feuilles,
et tombe exténué.
Sa connaissance est contrebande.

QUAND LE renne s'effondre
il dit 'renne':
voilà qu'il court parmi les lacs.
Quand le soleil fait ses adieux,
il dit 'soleil':
voilà qu'il écarte l'azur.
Quand le platane
n'est plus que bûche au coin du feu,
il dit 'platane':
le voilà recouvert de feuillage et d'oiseaux.
Quand les mots se suicident,
il ne dit aucun mot
et choisit le moins rare
—corde, abîme, poison—
pour mourir avec lui.

Notes for a Solitude

ALL CONSCIOUSNESS is mammalian, he says.
Like the urchin flight of the gull,
on everything
he puts his unpronounceable words.
The waters will stop.
The orange-trees will not go into exile.
Metals too hard
will house a patience.
He has some power:
like surf
washing up a tiny crab.

HE'S ON his own: like a defective verb.
Angles, volutes,
numbers, mirages
sometimes overcrowd him.
Like pups
he takes words on his lap
and pets them.
The month of May awaits him.
He runs under the leaves,
and falls exhausted.
His knowledge is contraband.

WHEN THE reindeer falls,
he says 'reindeer':
and it runs among the lakes.
When the sun takes its leave,
he says 'sun':
and it thrusts apart the blue.
When the planetree
is only a log at the fireside,
he says 'planetree':
and it grows leaves and birds.
When words commit suicide,
he speaks no word
and chooses the commonest
—rope, cliff, poison—
to die with it.

ENTRE LA pierre morte
et la statue qui chante
il est l'arbitre;
entre la lèvre
et le crâne défunt,
le temps trop incarné.
Il juge:
cet érable aurait tort de se croire un érable.
Il corrige un soleil
comme un devoir d'élève paresseux.
Il fera la morale
à la nuit qui commet le crime d'être nuit.
Il accepte pourtant la dictature
d'un scarabée qui boite.

ÉPOUVANTAIL au lieu de peau.
Chiffon brûlé à la place de l'âme.
Son aube tremble et se retire,
souris qui n'ose pas vivre parmi les hommes.
Il dort sous son plancher.
Il crie dans son placard.
Il n'est libre qu'au fond d'une serrure.
Deux potences,
un seul brin de muguet.

CHAIR à chair, page à page,
où vont les appétits
de l'âme qui confond
extase, indifférence, amour?
Il rédige une lettre
pour l'homme qu'il sera.
Tant d'énigmes frileuses!
Ombre à ombre, île à île,
où finiront
les images jetées
comme embryons dans la poubelle?
Il efface, il efface.
Sauvera-t-il la peau du doute?

BETWEEN dead stone
and singing statue
he is arbiter;
between lip
and lifeless skull,
all too incarnate time.
He judges:
this maple's wrong to call itself a maple.
He corrects the sun
like a lazy pupil's homework.
He'll preach morality
to night when it commits night.
Yet he accepts the dictates
of a limping beetle.

SCARECROW instead of skin.
Burnt rag in place of soul.
His dawn trembles and withdraws,
a mouse scared of living with men.
He sleeps under the floorboards.
He shouts in the cupboard.
He's only free inside a lock.
Two gibbets,
a single sprig of lily.

FLESH BY flesh, page by page,
where do the appetites go
of the soul confounding
ecstasy, indifference, love?
He composes a letter
to the man he will become.
So many chilly enigmas!
Shadow by shadow, island by island,
where will the images
end, thrown
in the garbage pail like foetuses?
He rubs out, rubs out.
Can he save doubt's skin?

PIERRE TORREILLES
Viens

PLUS BLANC que la nuit est le bleu
quand la lumière a rassemblé
l'ultime perfidie des pierres.
Sous l'insolence de leurs ruines,
hors de leurs ailes nul abri.

Fermes aux mains arrachées,
dans le soleil s'est répandue
la haute flambée des granges,
une volée de cloches a cloué les pigeons,
la barque d'un corbeau
cherche un abri puis meurt dans l'herbe;
les collines désamarrées
laissent survivre leur profil,
l'incendie de leurs toits exige plus d'espace.

Dans l'invisible démuni
les hommes parlent qui sont nés
à la lisière de leur deuil.
La tour feuillue garde la nuit
et des troupeaux, quand tout s'inverse
l'aube rejoint le crépuscule.

Le pas de Redortiers

FRANCHI LE col
dans l'ouverture enfin reconnais l'origine.
Encore errante la pensée,
de nulle ornière le sentier
redescendent au creux du monde.
Je savais le silence éclaté de l'oiseau
réduit à mille pierres.
Jette l'ombre aux mûres aveugles
la vallée s'ouvre renversée.
Franchi le pas, pierres comptées,
voici requise l'évidence:
arbres rares et mesurés.

Come

WHITER THAN night is the blue
when light has convened
the final treason of stones.
Under their ruins' arrogance,
from under their wings no shelter.

Farms torn from the grasp,
in sunlight spreads
the towering blaze of barns,
a volley of bells has nailed the pigeons,
the crow is a boat
seeking a haven then dying on the grass;
the hills cast their moorings,
survive in profile,
their blazing roofs demand more space.

In the helpless unseen
men talk who are born
on the verge of their mourning.
The leafy tower guards night
and flocks, when all's inverted
twilight and dawn unite.

The Pass of Redortiers

THROUGH THE pass, finally
at its mouth discern all origins.
Thought still astray
and a path without ruts
lead down to earth's centre.
I knew the bird's silence bursting
to a scatterment of stones.
Cast your shadow on the blind brambles,
the prostrate valley opens.
Through the pass, stones counted,
here is the proof required:
a few spaced-out trees.

Le retour

QUI EST-IL celui-là qui ne sait discerner
de la nuit ou du jour le rivage ?
celui que mesure l'approche,
depuis toujours gravé dans son silence.

Croix immobile il se tient à l'aplomb
imitant une tache du ciel,
traversé de lumière ; la mort seule le crée ;
En un cri retourné il souligne le bleu
et cloue midi sur son absence.
Lui, lumineux, porteur de l'ombre
surveillant du repos
la mort l'a rendu vertical.

Porteuse nue de la pluie
au lieu rassemblé d'absence
s'ouvre la pierre docile.

Dans les multiples pas des dieux,
la boue de l'aube ensevelie,
l'asphodèle déjà s'informe.

JEAN LAUDE
Le chemin de terre
A Jean Pierre et Marie-Odile Faye

TU NE sauras jamais où s'ouvre le chemin. Il s'ouvre d'un
    seul coup, dans la forêt confuse et se referme sur tes pas.
Tu ne sauras jamais où conduit le chemin. Longtemps tu mar-
    cheras. Longtemps, tu le suivras en sa clarté naissante. Et tu
    hésiteras.
La forêt qui le borde indique seulement qu'il y a un chemin.
    Son feuillage confus tremble d'ombres trouées.

Longtemps tu marcheras. Maintes fois, tu le suivras. Tu ne
    reconnaîtras jamais le seul chemin qui s'ouvre pour toi seul.
Sur chacun de tes pas, se ferme le chemin. L'oiseau crie et
    appelle. Il creuse un vide dans l'été. Il ouvre le chemin
    dans le tuf de l'été.
C'est un chemin de terre. Une forêt le borde. Et maintes fois,
    tu l'as foulé. Tu ne sauras jamais qu'il est le seul chemin.
    Que maintes fois tu l'as suivi.   *over*

The Return

WHO IS this that cannot distinguish
the shores of night and day?
who is measured by nearness,
for ever etched in silence.

Vertical cross, stock-still
he impersonates a patch of sky,
shot with light; death alone creates him;
Turned in a cry he affirms the blue
and nails midday upon its absence.
Himself, radiant, porter of shadow
guardian of rest
death has set him upright.

Naked rain-bearer
where absence masses
there opens the submissive rock.

In the countless steps of the gods,
dawn's mire entombed,
the asphodel asserts its question.

Earthway
To Jean Pierre and Marie-Odile Faye

YOU'LL NEVER know where the pathway opens. It opens at
a single stroke in the tangled forest and closes again on your
steps.
You'll never know where the pathway leads. For a long time
you'll walk. For a long time you'll follow it in its dawning
brightness. And you'll hesitate.
The forest flanking it shows only that there is a pathway. Its
tangled foliage trembles with tattered shadows.

For a long time you'll walk. Again and again you'll follow it.
You'll never recognize the only path that opens only for you.
On your every step the pathway closes. The bird cries and
calls. It creates an emptiness in the summer. It opens the
path in the stuff of summer.
It's an earthway. A forest flanks it. And you've trodden it
again and again. You'll never know that it's the only path-
way. That again and again you've followed it.

Où mène ce chemin, la clarté s'accomplit. Une maison s'étend
   contre l'épaule des collines.
Tu es venu de ce pays que l'horizon ferme trop tôt. Et main-
   tenant tu regardes l'espace.
A chacun de tes pas, recule la maison, recule la promesse, ô
   lointaine parole et toujours plus lointaine.

Tu as soif. Tu es altéré. L'oiseau est une source dans le tuf de
   l'été. Son chant désigne un vide en toi creusé.
Quel est cet autre, en toi, qui ne peut s'apaiser ? Sur le cri, sur
   l'appel, l'été lourd se referme.
Maintes fois, le chemin s'ouvrira et maintes fois encore tu
   marcheras, tu le suivras. Jusqu'à cette maison, jusqu'à cette
   parole—ô promesse lointaine et toujours plus lointaine
Qui t'illumine secrètement.

Lemmes

JE VIENS d'ici ou de là, dans l'ombre, et je marche.
Une vie à côté de la vie.
J'avance dans la marge où tombent les oiseaux. La frange où
   je me tiens ignore le sang mais connaît sa fadeur.
Une vie comme je hais, de nulle épaisseur. Le vide attablé.
   Les rideaux ont mangé ce qui reste d'éclats.
Le frange où je me tiens, c'est le sentier qui longe l'envers.

Qui appelle ?
               Une voix passe au-dessus de moi. Cette voix est
   risible. De l'autre côté, quelqu'un heurte des pierres et les
   déplace. Une voix demande un secours et cette voix est
   d'ailleurs. Quelqu'un m'appelle. C'est de l'autre côté. Je
   ne peux rien.

Le souci de vivre vaut aussi pour les autres—qui se taisent.

EN CETTE haute tour que tu as érigée,
En cette haute tour que de miroirs tu as murée,
Tu regardes de loin.

Tu regardes de loin ton image naissante,
Image fracturée que l'eau du fleuve emporte.   *over*

Where the path leads, brightness is accomplished. A house
stands against the hills' shoulder.
You have come from the country closed too soon by the
horizon. And now you look into space.
At your every step the house is further off, the promise further
off, O distant word ever more distant.

You are thirsty. You want to drink. The bird is a spring in the
soil of summer. Its song reveals an emptiness in yourself.
Who is the other, in you, who cannot be satisfied? On the cry,
on the call, sultry summer closes.
Again and again the pathway will open, again and again you'll
walk, you'll follow it. To the house, to the word—O distant
promise ever more distant
That is your secret light.

Lemmata

I COME from here or there, in shadow, and walk:
A life aside from life.
I go on into the margin where birds fall. The verge where I
stand knows nothing of blood, but knows its staleness.
The sort of life I hate, of no density. Emptiness sitting at table.
The curtains have eaten what's left of light.
The verge where I stand is the path beside the other side.

Who calls?
A voice passes above me. This voice is derisory.
On the other side, someone stumbles over stones and shifts
them. A voice asks for help and this voice is from elsewhere.
Someone calls me. It's from the other side. There's nothing
I can do.

Caring to live means something to others too—who keep silent.

IN THIS high tower you've built,
In this high tower you've walled with mirrors,
You gaze from a distance.

You gaze from a distance as your image is born,
Fragmented image borne away by the river's water.

Tu regardes de près le reflet des miroirs,
Ton image naissante dans l'eau gelée.

Tu ne vois plus le fleuve.
Non plus que ces miroirs.
Le fleuve, tu veux le remonter à sa source.
Tu veux traverser les miroirs.

Epousant cette image,
Une image naissante et reconstituée,
Te heurtant au miroir
Qui te cache le fleuve.

Ne pouvant épouser cette image
Illusoire et privée,
La simple image prisonnière
Qui ne t'appartient plus,

Tu te heurtes aux murs que tu as érigés,
Captive d'une image
Que tu ne peux épouser.

JEAN-CLAUDE RENARD
L'hiver autour du sang

LE SOL, dans le verger, m'incorpore à ses boues.
Je fais le tour des arbres que le brouillard entoure en
bougeant avec moi.
Tourne sous une branche immobile et glacée comme une
arme ancienne
Et remonte mes pas sans avoir rien rejoint
Que le même ciment—que le même silence.
Mais un peu de lavande a brûlé sur la pierre et le seuil a
changé.
Ce bois mort, ces feuillages desséchés dans la grange,
Il me semble à présent qu'ils ne se soient éteints que pour
laisser en moi surgir cette racine
Qui recréera le feu dont ils seront la force.
Et si, devant la vitre où s'annonce la neige, je puis toucher
un peu la nuit purifiée,
Je ferais naître enfin le soleil qui l'habite.

You gaze closely at the mirrors' reflection,
Your image born in the frozen water.

You no longer see the river.
Or the mirrors.
The river you want to retrace to its source.
You want to pass through the mirrors.

Uniting with the image,
Image born and recreated,
You are baulked by the mirror
That hides the river.

Unable to unite with the illusory
And private image,
The mere captive image
That is no longer yours,

You are baulked by the walls you have built,
Captive of an image
With which you cannot unite.

The Winter round the Blood

THE EARTH in the orchard blends me with its mud.
I walk through trees wrapped in fog that moves with me.
Turn below a branch motionless and frozen as an antique
weapon
And retrace my steps having met nothing
But the same bonding, the same silence.
But a little lavender has burned on the stone and the
threshold has changed.
This dead wood, those dried-up leaves in the barn,
I feel now they burned out only to let this root grow in me
That will recreate the fire whose strength they will be.
And if, at the window where snow promises, I can touch
the purified night,
I should at last bring to birth the sun that inhabits it.

J'invoquerai le fleuve

QUELQU'UN EST venu tôt,
Parmi les tournesols,
Laissant dans un panier des citrons et du pain.
Une lueur lointaine—et nulle plus intime
Au delà des falaises
Indiquait le chemin de quelles transhumances.
Il y avait dans l'air
Un goût de chèvrefeuille.
J'ai marché jusqu'au fleuve—et l'odeur de la laine était
un chien obscur.
L'autre bord du secret nous a-t-il entendus ?
Quel silence pressent qu'un mystère s'élit
Dans cette angoisse même d'un sens et d'un amour,
Cette crainte sous l'arbre, cette fascination de la
profonde source là-bas, derrière l'aube et derrière la mort,
Dont s'éclairent les bois,
Ce désir d'absolu chargé déjà du sang qui donne
ressemblance,
—Ce froid sacré où prend l'inaccessible feu ?

La limite des cendres

J'AI RAPPORTÉ du bois.

Le feu ne franchit pas la limite des cendres
Mais la chaleur du feu pénètre la maison.

Une fente s'est faite dans les briques glacées,
La barrière d'absence.
Une fourrure d'air pour les membres, les meubles,
La nudité de l'âme.

Il y a maintenant comme une ombre éclairée
Dans l'angle de la nuit,
Un début de lumière, presque un pont transparent
D'une île à l'autre.
Quelque chose de pur qui commence à parler plus bas que
la parole
Mais dit peut-être plus.
Ce que déjà je trouve,
Ce que déjà je touche
Me perd en me brûlant.   *over*

I Shall Invoke the River

SOMEONE CAME early
Among the sunflowers,
Leaving bread and lemons in a basket.
A far-off glow—and none more intimate
Beyond the cliffs
Showed the way for what migrating flocks.
In the air
A taste of honeysuckle.
I walked to the river—and the smell of wool was a dog
obscurely.
Did the other bank of the secret hear us?
What silence divines that a mystery is being chosen
In this anguish for meaning and love,
This fear under the tree, this fascination for the deep spring
far off, behind dawn, behind death,
Lighting the woods,
This immortal longing already gorged with the blood that
confers likeness
—This sacred cold where the inaccessible fire takes hold?

Edge of the Ashes

I'VE BROUGHT in logs.

The fire doesn't overstep the ashes
But its heat fills the house.

A crack has opened in the frozen bricks,
Barrier of absence.
A fur-coat of air for limbs, furniture,
Naked soul.

A shadow now seems lit
In night's corner,
An onset of light, a transparent bridge almost
From one island to the other.
A purity starting to speak softer than speech
But perhaps with more to say.
What now I find,
What now I touch
Burns and destroys me.

Est-ce plus loin que luit la substance fruitée
Qui laisse s'unifier la rivière et la braise
Sans que rien ne s'altère de l'une ni de l'autre ?

Un vide en moi s'avive—où vient sourdre un appel formé
pour la réponse et pour l'unique essence
De ce qui l'a créé.
L'arbre même soudain, dans le néant fertile, dans l'espace
du temps qui ne peut s'accomplir qu'avec l'éternité,
M'est libre et nécessaire
Et son mystère attend que je le sois pour lui.

J'allumerai son nom
Dans cette mort ouverte où l'invisible été prend la
douceur des seins.

Si l'arbre prenait nom

Il n'y a pas de vent.

Ce pin sur la falaise
Se demeure étranger et me demeure absent.

Le bois d'avant la neige portait peut-être un nom
Suffisant et fidèle où les oiseaux luisaient.

Le bois d'après le feu connaîtra-t-il la mer ?

Je ne vois dans la nuit que le profil des branches
—Leur repos et leur soif.

Quelle tête immobile et qui convie la lune
Attend devant mes os,
Approche de ma bouche son silence aimanté ?

Une menace saigne entre ma mort et lui.

Une odeur de résine plus douce que le bruit des colombes
qui boivent
Invite à nidifier dans ce puits fascinant.

C'est l'arbre si je parle !

Lui et moi mêlés d'or
Et dressés l'un dans l'autre comme avec une femme.

Mais l'écorce est pierreuse et froide sous mes mains.   *over*

Does the substance, syrup-sweet, glow more distant
Allowing flame and river to unite
Without changing either?

An emptiness in me springs alive—an appeal demanding
reply and the single essence
Of what created it.
Suddenly even the tree, in fertile absence, in time's
space that only eternity can fill,
Is free and indispensable to me
And its mystery waits: when shall I be so to the tree?

I shall light its name
Here in this gaping death where sweet as breasts
invisible summer comes.

If the Tree took a Name

THERE IS no wind.

The pinetree on the cliff
Is a stranger to itself and absent to me.

The wood before snow bore perhaps
A faithful and adequate name where birds flickered.

Will the wood after fire know the sea?

I can see in the night only the branches' outline
—Their repose and their thirst.

What motionless head calling on the moon
Waits before my bones,
Its magnet silence nearing my lips?

A threat bleeds between it and my death.

A smell of resin sweeter than the sound of doves drinking
Calls to build a nest in this mesmeric well.

It's the tree if I speak!

It and I mingled with gold
And erect in each other as with a woman.

But the bark is cold and stony under my hands.

Ce mal que j'ai formé de mon propre refus et croyais
emmuré dans mes seules cavernes
   Est maintenant ici et au dehors de moi comme un lierre
noué à chaque lierre noir
   Et qui croît avec eux
   Pour revenir en moi, chargé de quels pouvoirs plus
anciens encore,
   Lier plus fortement ce qui me retient d'être !

Un rameau éloigné tombe dans les ténèbres.

FAUT-IL trouver dans la nuit
Et dans la distance qui dure à l'intérieur de l'amour
Sous d'épaisses couches d'acides
Quelqu'un présent par absence ?

Il n'y a rien pour convaincre
Ce sable opaque où l'eau glace
Et n'est plus propre au partage
Sinon qu'aucun silence n'annule le mystère.

Essayant de peupler la mort
Le sang invente, prophétise,
Voit parfois luire dans la neige comme un grand cerf ressuscité
Le sacre dont l'hiver le fascine et le tue.

Mais peut-être qu'à l'aube, après tant d'arbres vides,
Le dieu sera vivant.

PRÈS DU puits, sous la glume,
Des taupes agonisent
Et les radis sont secs comme des scarabées
Dans le sable apporté par les vents anciens.
   Ce soir encore, des meutes venues du brûlis ont dévasté
les meules soustraites à la foudre.
   Une étrange insistance
   (Difficile à saisir tant il faut, pour l'atteindre ici, dans la
chair même, apprendre à se donner)
   Indique qu'une issue doit pourtant exister dans les
cavernes mortes,   *over*

This evil I have shaped from my refusal and walled up,
I thought, in my caverns
    Now stands here outside me like an ivy knotted into each
black ivy
    Growing with them
    To re-enter me, charged with what even older powers,
    To bind more strongly what holds me from being!

A distant bough falls in the darkness.

Is IT in night we must find
And in the distance perpetuated within love
Under dense layers of acid
Someone present by absence?

There is nothing to convince
This opaque sand where water freezes
And is no longer suited to division
Except that no silence annuls the mystery.

Trying to people death
Blood invents, prophesies,
Sees sometimes shining in the snow like a great stag revived
The rite whose winter fascinates and kills it.

But perhaps at dawn, after so many empty trees,
The god will be alive.

NEAR THE well, beneath the chaff,
Moles are dying
And radishes brittle as beetles
In the sand that bygone winds have drifted.
    This evening again, packs out of the burnt lands ravaged
the hayricks lightning had spared.
    A strange insistency
    (Hard to grasp, for to grasp it here, here in the body, hard
you must learn to yield)
    Points to a way existing out of these lifeless caverns

L'étouffement de l'être fait pour les hautes fêtes.
    Mais si la neige tombe avant que le dieu parle,—
chassant les fanatismes,
    Qui gardera pouvoir de soulever ces pierres terribles et
désertes
    Pour écouter mûrir avec l'eau, dans les arbres,
    Le tintement de l'air ?

YVES BONNEFOY
Douve parle

I. QUELQUEFOIS, DISAIS-TU, errante à l'aube
Sur des chemins noircis,
Je partageais l'hypnose de la pierre,
J'étais aveugle comme elle.
Or est venu ce vent par quoi mes comédies
Se sont élucidées en l'acte de mourir.

Je désirais l'été,
Un furieux été pour assécher mes larmes,
Or est venu ce froid qui grandit dans mes membres,
Et je fus éveillée et je souffris.

II. O fatale saison,
O terre la plus nue comme une lame !
Je désirais l'été,
Qui a rompu ce fer dans le vieux sang ?

Vraiment je fus heureuse
A ce point de mourir.
Les yeux perdus, mes mains s'ouvrant à la souillure
D'une éternelle pluie.

Je criais, j'affrontais de ma face le vent . . .
Pourquoi haïr, pourquoi pleurer, j'étais vivante,
L'été profond, le jour me rassuraient.

III. Que le verbe s'éteigne
Sur cette face de l'être où nous sommes exposés,
Sur cette aridité que traverse
Le seul vent de finitude.

Que celui qui brûlait debout
Comme une vigne,   *over*

Where the being stifles, created for high festivity.
But if snow falls before the god speaks—driving out
bigotries—
Who'll still find strength to lift aside those stones
of desert fear
To hear with the water, in the trees, ripen
The air's pealing?

Douve Speaks

I. SOMETIMES, YOU said, wandering at dawn
On darkened paths,
I shared in stone's hypnosis,
was blind like stone.
Then came this wind by which my comedies
Grew lucid in the act of dying.

I longed for summer,
A raging summer that would dry my tears,
Then came this cold increasing in my limbs,
And I was awakened and I suffered.

II. O deadly season,
O earth most bare like a blade!
I longed for summer,
Who broke this lance in ancient blood?

Truly I was happy
To the point of dying.
Eyes lost, hands open to pollution
Of eternal rain.

I shouted out, turned my face to the wind . . .
Why hate, why weep, I was alive,
The deep midsummer, the daylight reassured me.

III. Let the word be snuffed out
This side of existence where we are exposed,
On this barrenness swept
By the wind of finitude.

Let him who burned erect
Like a vine,

Que l'extrême chanteur roule de la crête
Illuminant
L'immense matière indicible.

Que le verbe s'éteigne
Dans cette pièce basse où tu me rejoins,
Que l'âtre du cri se resserre
Sur nos mots rougeoyants.

Que le froid par ma mort se lève et prenne un sens.

Lieu de la salamandre

LA SALAMANDRE surprise s'immobilise
Et feint la mort.
Tel est le premier pas de la conscience dans les pierres,
Le mythe le plus pur,
Un grand feu traversé, qui est esprit.

La salamandre était à mi-hauteur
Du mur, dans la clarté de nos fenêtres.
Son regard n'était qu'une pierre,
Mais je voyais son cœur battre éternel.

O ma complice et ma pensée, allégorie
De tout ce qui est pur,
Que j'aime qui resserre ainsi dans son silence
La seule force de joie.

Que j'aime qui s'accorde aux astres par l'inerte
Masse de tout son corps,
Que j'aime qui attend l'heure de sa victoire,
Et qui retient son souffle et tient au sol.

La beauté

CELLE QUI ruine l'être, la beauté,
Sera suppliciée, mise à la roue,
Déshonorée, dite coupable, faite sang
Et cri, et nuit, de toute joie dépossédée
—O déchirée sur toutes grilles d'avant l'aube,
O piétinée sur toute route et traversée,
Notre haut désespoir sera que tu vives,
Notre cœur que tu souffres, notre voix   *over*

Let the ultimate singer fall from the hilltop
Lighting up
Matter immense and unsayable.

Let the word be snuffed out
In this cramped room where you join me,
Let the hearth of the cry contract
Upon our glowing words.

Let cold by my death rise up and take on meaning.

Place of the Salamander

THE SALAMANDER caught unawares freezes
And imitates death.
Such is the first step of awareness in the stones,
The purest myth,
Journey through a great fire, which is spirit.

The salamander was halfway up
The wall, in the light from our windows.
Its gaze was no more than a stone,
But I saw its heart beating eternal.

O my accomplice and my thought, allegory
Of all that is pure,
That I love that clenches in its silence
The solitary power of joy.

That I love that concords with planets by the inert
Mass of its total substance,
That I love that awaits the hour of its victory,
Holding its breath, clinging to solid earth.

Beauty

SHE THAT destroys being, beauty,
Shall be tortured, strapped to the wheel,
Dishonoured, called guilty, made blood
And cry, and night, of all joy dispossessed
—O torn apart on all before-dawn gridirons,
O trampled on every road and crossing,
Our high despair shall be that you live,
Our heart that you suffer, our voice

De t'humilier parmi tes larmes, de te dire
La menteuse, la pourvoyeuse du ciel noir,
Notre désir pourtant étant ton corps infirme,
Notre pitié ce cœur menant à toute boue.

Le pays découvert

L'ÉTOILE SUR le seuil. Le vent, tenu
Dans les mains immobiles de la mort.
La parole et le vent furent de longue lutte,
Puis le silence vint dans le calme du vent.

Le pays découvert était de pierre grise.
Très bas, très loin gisait l'éclair d'un fleuve nul.
Mais les pluies de la nuit sur la terre surprise
Ont réveillé l'ardeur que tu nommes le temps.

Ici, toujours ici

ICI, DANS le lieu clair. Ce n'est plus l'aube,
C'est déjà la journée aux dicibles désirs.
Des mirages d'un chant dans ton rêve il ne reste
Que ce scintillement de pierres à venir.

Ici, et jusqu'au soir. La rose d'ombres
Tournera sur les murs. La rose d'heures
Défleurira sans bruit. Les dalles claires
Mèneront à leur gré ces pas épris du jour.

Ici, toujours ici. Pierres sur pierres
Ont bâti le pays dit par le souvenir.
A peine si le bruit de fruits simples qui tombent
Enfièvre encore en toi le temps qui va guérir.

ANDRÉ DU BOUCHET
Flot

JE SUIS saisi par le coude noir
tout s'efface

l'arbre
ce qu'il y a de bestial   *over*

To humiliate you among your tears, to call you
The cheat, the purveyor of black sky,
Our desire being still your frail body,
Our pity this heart leading to muddy ends.

The Land Revealed

STAR ON the threshold. Wind, held
In the motionless hands of death.
Speech and the wind were long in contest,
Then came silence in the wind's calm.

The land revealed was of grey stone.
Far down, far off lay the lightning of a cancelled river.
But the rains of night on the surprised earth
Have awakened the ardour that you call time.

Here, Still Here

HERE, IN the place of brightness. It is no longer dawn,
It is already the daytime of admissible desires.
Of the mirages of song in your dreaming, remains
Only this glinting of future stones.

Here, and till evening. The rose of shadows
Will turn on the walls. The rose of hours
Will soundlessly shed its petals. The bright flagstones
Will lead as they will these steps in love with daylight.

Here, still here. Stone upon stone
Has built the country spoken by memory.
Barely the sound of fruit falling one by one
Enfevers you again with time: time will be cured.

Flood

I AM gripped by the black elbow
everything's obliterated

the tree
all that is bestial

le feu gagne lentement les espaces froids
les chaises au port sur les lames immobiles

lampe muselée

la chambre qui avait croulé avec toi
sans mot dire
au bout de quelque temps s'est remise à parler

en hiver.

Cession

LE VENT,
            dans les terres sans eau de l'été, nous quitte sur une
    lame,
        ce qui subsiste du ciel.
En plusieurs fractures, la terre se précise. La terre demeure
stable dans le souffle qui nous dénude.

Ici, dans le monde immobile et bleu, j'ai presque atteint ce mur.
Le fond du jour est encore devant nous. Le fond embrasé de la
terre. Le fond et la surface du front,
                                aplani par le même souffle,
ce froid.

Je me recompose au pied de la façade comme l'air bleu au
pied des labours.

                Rien ne désaltère mon pas.

ROGER GIROUX
From *Décrire le paysage*

LA COULEUR de la mer est semblable au matin.
Le ciel est plein d'oiseaux que le vent a laissés.
Des navires sont là, des bateaux et des barques.
Et les fruits, calmes,
Attendent que l'été leur donne la lumière.

Et nous allons, par l'invisible porte.
Et dans les grandes vallées bleues du coeur
Où la mémoire n'atteint pas
Une voile s'approche, entre les apparences,
Et fait signe de taire le nom du paysage.

over

fire slowly invades the cold spaces
chairs in the harbour on motionless waves

muzzled lamp

the room that collapsed with you
wordlessly
after a time began to speak again

in winter.

Cession

WIND,
  in the waterless lands of summer, deserts us in a
 blade,
   what stays of sky.
In fragments, the earth becomes clearer. The earth remains
stable in the breath that strips us.

Here, in the motionless blue world, I have almost reached that
wall. The depth of day is still before us. The scorched depth of
the earth. The depth and surface of the forehead,
      smoothed by the same breath,
this cold.

I recompose myself at the foot of the façade like the blue air
at the foot of the ploughed fields.

      Nothing satiates my step.

THE SEA is morning-coloured,
The sky full of birds left by the wind.
There are ships, boats and trawlers.
And the fruits, serene,
Wait for summer to give them light.

And we go, through the unseen door.
And in the big blue valleys of the heart
Where memory cannot reach
A sail approaches, between appearances,
And signs to us to conceal this country's name.

Et les arbres s'éloignent dans l'automne
Et recouvrent nos pas de leurs vagues mourantes.
Une ombre va, dans les collines,
Et puis, que reste-t-il de ce pays, qu'un peu de neige
Qui tombe, dans le creux de la main ?

L'impossible silence accomplit son espace,
Et voici, lentement, mon image détruite.
Mes yeux perdent le souvenir,
Et mon visage meurt, de miroir, d'absence,
Comme, au bord de la branche, un songe dans sa fleur.

NUE,
Frileusement venue,
Devenue elle sans raison, ne sachant
Quel simulacre de l'amour appeler en image
(belle d'un doute inachevé
vague après vague,
et comme inadvenue aux lèvres), ici
d'une autre qui n'est plus
que sa feinte substance nommée

Miroir, abusive nacelle,
eau de pur silex.

PHILIPPE JACCOTTET

SOIS TRANQUILLE, cela viendra ! Tu te rapproches,
tu brûles ! Car le mot qui sera à la fin
du poème, plus que le premier sera proche
de ta mort, qui ne s'arrête pas en chemin.

Ne crois pas qu'elle aille s'endormir sous des branches
ou reprendre souffle pendant que tu écris.
Même quand tu bois à la bouche qui étanche
la pire soif, la douce bouche avec ses cris

doux, même quand tu serres avec force le nœud
de vos quatre bras pour être bien immobiles
dans la brûlante obscurité de vos cheveux,

elle vient, Dieu sait par quels détours, vers vous deux,
de très loin ou déjà tout près, mais sois tranquille,
elle vient : d'un à l'autre mot tu es plus vieux.

And the trees are distanced by autumn
And cover our steps with their dying waves.
A shadow goes, in the hills,
And then what is left of this land, but a little snow
Falling in the palm of the hand?

Impossible silence achieves its space,
And here, slowly, is my ruined image.
My eyes lose their memory,
And my face dies, of mirror, of absence,
Like, at the branch's edge, a dream in flower.

NAKED,
Shiveringly come,
Become for no reason herself, not knowing
What semblance of love to call upon for image
(beautiful with imperfect doubt
vague upon vague,
and as if uncome to the lips), here and now
of another existing no longer
but as named pretended substance

Mirror, deceptive cradle,
water of pure flint.

DON'T WORRY, it'll come! You're warmer, yes,
you're getting close! The poem's very last
word will be closer than the first to death
who never breaks his journey for a rest.

Don't think that while you're writing this he takes
a breather, forty winks, still less a seat.
And even when you drink the mouth that slakes
the driest thirst, the sweet mouth with its sweet

Cries, even when you lie in hiding there
and you draw tight the knot of your four arms
passionately, take cover in your hair,

He comes, God knows the long way round he comes:
far off, or else perhaps (but never fear:
you age from one word to the next) he's near.

Portovenere

LA MER est de nouveau obscure. Tu comprends,
c'est la dernière nuit. Mais qui vais-je appelant ?
Hors l'écho, je ne parle à personne, à personne.
Où s'écroulent les rocs, la mer est noire, et tonne
dans sa cloche de pluie. Une chauve-souris
cogne aux barreaux de l'air d'un vol comme surpris,
tous ces jours sont perdus, déchirés par ses ailes
noires, la majesté de ces eaux trop fidèles
me laisse froid, puisque je ne parle toujours
ni à toi, ni à rien. Qu'ils sombrent, ces 'beaux jours' !
Je pars, je continue à vieillir, peu m'importe,
sur qui s'en va la mer saura claquer la porte.

TOUTE FLEUR n'est que de la nuit
qui feint de s'être rapprochée

Mais là d'où son parfum s'élève
je ne puis espérer entrer
c'est pourquoi tant il me trouble
et me fait si longtemps veiller
devant cette porte fermée

Toute couleur, toute vie
naît d'où le regard s'arrête

Ce monde n'est que la crête
d'un invisible incendie

TOUT À LA FIN de la nuit
quand ce souffle s'est élevé
une bougie d'abord
a défailli

Avant les premiers oiseaux
qui peut encore veiller ?
Le vent le sait, qui traverse les fleuves

Cette flamme, ou larme inversée:
une obole pour le passeur

Portovenere

THE SEA is dark again. You understand,
this is the last night. But who am I calling?
Echo apart, I speak to no-one, no-one.
Where the rocks tumble, the sea is black, and booming
in its bell of rain. A bat
as if caught in flight knocks against bars of air,
all these days are lost, torn by its black
wings, the majesty of this too predictable water
leaves me cold, since still I address
neither you nor anything. Let these 'happy days' all founder!
To depart, or go on ageing, what's the difference?
Behind my back the sea will slam the door.

ANY FLOWER is but night
pretending to draw close

But the source of its perfume
I cannot hope to enter
this is why it so much troubles me
and makes me watch so long
before that closed door

All colour, all life
is born where the gaze stops

This world is but the crest
of an invisible fire

AT CLOSE of night
when this breath sighed
a candle first
guttered

Before the first birds
who still keeps vigil?
The wind that crosses rivers knows

This flame, or inverted tear:
an obol for the ferryman

JE NE veux plus me poser
voler à la vitesse du temps

croire ainsi un instant
mon attente immobile

PEU M'IMPORTE le commencement du monde

Maintenant ses feuilles bougent
maintenant c'est un arbre immense
dont je touche le bois navré

Et la lumière à travers lui
brille de larmes

ROBERT MARTEAU
Métamorphose des amants

DE PARTOUT la nuit craque et se fend
Et les amants se retrouvent couverts de plume
Avec un peu de sable sur les doigts.

Les amants ont soif dans leur lit desséché
Car toute l'eau est partie se noyer dans la mer;
Et les coqs à la fenêtre se poussent du jabot
Picorant dans la vitre les dernières étoiles.

Amants qui portez des panaches blancs et des couteaux
Saignez ces coqs et dans un plat de faïence
Répandez leur sang: qu'ils dorment, qu'ils dorment
Dans le cercle de craie où vos bras les ont clos.

From *Travaux pour un bûcher*

MASQUÉ DE bronze,
Uni dans l'antre aux mâcheuses de pavots,
Guêtré des squames du Python,
Coiffé de phoque, barbouillé de vendange,
Dompteur de chevaux, voleur de bœufs,
Sous la triple apparence,
Linguistes, grammairiens n'ont pas su le surprendre,
Mais si ceux qui chiquent, ceux qui goinfrent le patois,
Voyeurs, voyous qui perdent la santé dans le marc et la gnôle;

over

I WANT never again to settle
but fly at the speed of time

and so believe for a moment
my waiting motionless

NEVER MIND the beginning of the world

Now its leaves move
now it's an immense tree
whose disconsolate wood I touch

And the light through it
glistens with tears

Metamorphosis of Lovers

ON EVERY side the night cracks and splits open
And the lovers wake covered in feathers
A little sand on their fingers.

The lovers are thirsty in their dried-up bed
For all the water has gone to be drowned in the sea;
And the cocks at the window jostle crop to crop
Pecking the last stars out of the glass.

Lovers who wear white feathers and knives
Bleed those cockerels and in an earthenware dish
Smear their blood: let them sleep, let them sleep
In the chalk circle where your arms have shut them.

From Project for a Funeral Pyre

MASKED WITH bronze,
Joined in the cavern with the poppy-chewers,
Gaitered with the Python's scales,
Capped with sealskin, smeared with grape-juice,
Tamer of horses, stealer of oxen,
Under the triple aspect,
Linguists, grammarians could not glimpse him,
But those who chew quids, or gorge on dialect,
Peeping toms, no-goods who wreck their health on brandy
    and hooch;

Quand ils sont saouls,
Voyants qui prennent pour le ciel les poutres du plafond.
Empennés de velours j'en ai vu la corde au cou
Monter en sainte extase, au clou lier l'échelle :
Passait devant leurs yeux l'aile teinte d'euphorbe,
Orbes évacués
Dont la trajectoire raye les cartes du couchant.

Mais moi que cet amour obsède je reviens
à l'envers sur les pas d'Alexandre et ne cède
à nul percheron la part du labeur—les biens
oui—qui n'étreins à l'extrême qu'un corps de cendre.

J'entends depuis des siècles les charpentiers
qui clouent les échafauds et dressent les potences
empoignent la varlope arpentent le chantier
s'essuient la moustache où la sueur se condense.

Bleu marine la nuit déteint sur les chevaux
entravés parmi les boutons d'or. Les noyaux
d'olives que nous crachons dans l'eau du Scamandre

à peine trouent le monde où les morts vont descendre.
Le marbre est plus beau que les mouches ont rongé
enfin la rose germe où l'orgueil fut logé.

O morts à vous tout de suite qu'on se voue.
A vous je pense, à vous, Eternel Pharaon,
Dont les yeux me détournent du temps,
Et sur la cuirasse du scarabée
Seule de l'azur au noir la lumière joue.

Voyez, à force de compter les étoiles,
Ils ont appris à paître leurs agneaux ;
Ils savent quand l'urne qui s'incline
Sur la terre versera son eau.

Un seul que les Muses désignent
Aura pouvoir d'assembler les mots :
L'une lui dicte les lignes,
L'autre les ébarbe aux ciseaux.

Ainsi s'enchaînent à l'homme
Les divines, les cruelles,   *over*

When they're drunk,
Seers who see heaven in the beams of the ceiling.
Velvet-pinioned I've seen them, a rope round their necks,
Climbing in holy ecstasy, hitching the ladder to a nail:
A wing tinged with spurge passed before their eyes,
Empty sockets,
Orbit-stroke across the maps of sunset.

But I obsessed by this love retrace
the steps of Alexander in reverse and to
no plough-horse yield the share of labour—the profit
yes—embracing at the end only a body of ash.

I can hear the carpenters nailing up
scaffolds for centuries, setting up the gallows
gripping the plane treading the workshop floor
wiping congealing sweat from their beards.

Navy-blue night rubs off on the horses
hobbled in the buttercups. The olive-stones
we spit into Scamander's water

make hardly a dent in the world where the dead will go.
Marble is finer that is fly-blown
the rose at last seeds where pride dwelt.

Now to the dead let us vow ourselves.
To you, I think of you, Immortal Pharaoh,
Whose eyes avert me from time,
And on the scarab shell
Only light playing from azure to black.

See, by counting the stars,
They have learnt to pasture their lambs;
They know when the tipping urn
Will spill its water on the ground.

Only one appointed by the Muses
Will have power to assemble the words:
One dictates his lines,
The other trims them with scissors.

Thus are linked to Man
The divine, the cruel,

Les abominables et belles prostituées
Pareilles parfois à celles
Des music-halls que poursuivent les veufs
A l'envers du rideau.

Barge sur les eaux: Spiritus Sanctus!
A vous de calculer la dérive,
A vous de nous dire
Quand reviendra l'oiseau
Qui parut en Egypte
Et qui était le fils et qui était le père
De celui qui ressuscite
Quand l'autre brûle sur l'autel.

Véronique

CE JUILLET de chiffon rouge n'a pas fini
De boucher ma mémoire, et seul était fleuri
Le laurier; plus d'oiseaux, rien que paille; l'écume
M'incisait les yeux; un astre, un phare s'allume.

Lugubre bête, un monde a gîté pour la nuit,
Tassé, la dent longue; un monde, un énorme fruit
D'échardes, bogue, noix, herse ou serpent à plumes
De fer, silencieux comme un centre d'enclume.

Il y eut cette crête en haut des lys de mer
Et dans l'esprit de sel ce voyage de noces,
Des transhumances, des élus au sacerdoce

Ouvrant d'immenses fleurs, parcourant des déserts.
Il y eut ce visage essuyé, ce visage
Imprimé dans l'étoffe—en vrai, en témoignage.

Sibylla Sambetha

2

J'AIME QUE les bûcherons allument un grand feu
dans la hêtraie quand je mets le mot automne
     sur ma page
et qu'en fourrure la fumée bleue festoie.

     Haches et ramiers
à coups d'aile éparpillent les copeaux: *over*

The foul and beautiful whores
Sometimes resembling those
Of the music-halls whom widowers pursue
The other side of the curtain.

Barge on the waters: Spiritus Sanctus!
Yours to compute the drift,
Yours to inform us
When the bird will return
That appeared in Egypt
And was son and was father
Of the bird reborn
When the other is burnt on the altar.

Veronica

STILL THAT red rag July
Sticks in my memory, and only the laurel
Was flowering; no more birds, only straw; foam
Lanced my eyes; a star, a headlight switches on.

A sullen, animal world dossed down for the night,
Hunched, long-toothed; a fat fruit world
Of splinters, burr, nut, harrow or iron-plumed
Serpent, silent as an anvil centre.

There was a crest above the sea-lilies
And in the salt spirit a honeymoon,
Moving of flocks, priesthood's elect

Opening huge flowers, trekking over deserts.
There was a face wiped dry, a face
Printed in the linen—as truth, as a witness.

Sibylla Sambetha

2
I LIKE the bonfire lit by woodcutters
in the beech-wood when I write autumn
    on my page
and the fur-festive billow of blue smoke.

    Ring-doves' and axes'
wing-blows scatter the twigs:

pourpre sur la terre, Rome répandue,
et moi liant les rames en fagot
    à d'autres temps je dévoue
la cire blanche où l'abeille nidifie.

3
Plus de braise au trépied
et j'ignore si les serpents
qui prolongent ici leur veille
gardent en bouche sac et dent

et s'ils sauraient sur la pierre sacrale
    délover le foetus,
s'accroître verticalement
vers les hautes cuves lactées.

Serpents qu'émerveilla la baguette,
loin des oranges le retrait,
    et dans l'écume
quel œuf à couver ?

4
Vous ne viendrez plus. Le troëne
    et les vitres du train
depuis ont effacé le visage
et le chiffon que juin copiait.

Amandes sur la terre, pluie :
    il faisait si beau
que le pays s'est cassé.

De la bouche des sibylles,
moi-même entendrais-je la parole
quand c'est le retrait que je vois
    de toute flamme ?
et rien ne brûle—mais si, peut-être
    ce pan de sable
comme on dit un lit de noces.

Ancienne guerre, forfait futur :
    au milieu de la meute
quelqu'un tombe, ici,
en pleine fleur printanière
et dans l'herbe du verger.

over

purple on the ground, spilt Rome,
and I binding the branches into faggots
   vow to other times
the white wax, the bee's nest.

3
No more fire for the tripod
and I do not know if the snakes
prolonging their vigil here
have jaws still sharp with sac and fang

and if on the ritual stone they could
   uncoil the foetus,
rear erect
towards the high milk-vats.

Snakes mesmerized by the rod,
retreat far from oranges
   and in the foam
what egg to hatch?

4
You'll not come now. Privet
   and train-windows
have long since effaced the face
and the cloth's June copy.

Almonds on the ground, rain:
   the weather so fine
the countryside broke.

From the sibyls' lips
would even I hear the word
now that I see retreat
   of every flame?
and nothing burns—or yes, perhaps
   this patch of sand,
a marriage-bed almost.

Bygone war, havoc to come:
   in the midst of the pack
someone falls, here,
in full spring flower
and in the orchard grass.

A cause de la lutte des classes
le boucher tend sur l'étal
    sa toile rouge rayée
bien que le sang ne l'effraie pas
non plus que la viande morte.

JACQUES DUPIN
Grand vent

NOUS N'APPARTENONS qu'au sentier de montagne
Qui serpente au soleil entre la sauge et le lichen
Et s'élance à la nuit, chemin de crête,
A la rencontre des constellations.
Nous avons rapproché des sommets
La limite des terres arables.
Les graines éclatent dans nos poings.
Les flammes rentrent dans nos os.
Que le fumier monte à dos d'hommes jusqu'à nous !
Que la vigne et le seigle répliquent
A la vieillesse du volcan !
Les fruits de l'orgueil, les fruits du basalte
Mûriront sous les coups
Qui nous rendent visibles.
La chair endurera ce que l'œil a souffert,
Ce que les loups n'ont pas rêvé
Avant de descendre à la mer.

L'urne

SANS FIN regarder poindre une seconde nuit
A travers cet inerte bûcher lucide
Que ne tempère aucune production de cendres.

Mais la bouche à la fin, la bouche pleine de terre
Et de fureur,
Se souvient que c'est elle qui brûle
Et guide les berceaux sur le fleuve.

Le cœur par défaut

UNE FLEUR de givre entre deux rafales
Ne l'arrête pas.

over

Because of the class struggle
the butcher's stall displays
   his red streaked cloth
though blood worries him
no more than dead meat.

High Wind

WE BELONG only to the mountain path
Winding in sunlight between sage and lichen
And hastening to darkness, mountain-top road,
To meet the constellations.
We have brought the edge of our cornfields
Close to the summits.
The grains burst in our hands.
The flames enter our bones.
Let men shoulder the dung and carry it up here.
Let wine and ryebread answer
The age of the volcano.
The fruits of pride, the fruits of basalt
Will ripen under the blows
That make us visible.
Flesh will endure what eyes have suffered,
What wolves have not dreamed
Before descending to the sea.

The Urn

ENDLESSLY WATCHING a second night dawning
Through this passive and lucid pyre
Cooled by no produce of ash.

But the mouth after all, the mouth filled with earth
And frenzy,
Remembers what burns is itself
And guides the cradles on the river.

The Heart by Default

A FLOWER of frost between two gusts
Don't check it.

O cendre éprise sous la langue,
Brèche dans l'horizon !

Entre ce roc bondé d'étoiles et son sosie le gouffre,
L'édifice du souffle est une seconde prison.

A la place du cœur
Tu ne heurteras, mon amour, que le luisant d'un soc
Et la nuit grandissante . . .

Le palimpseste

LES CRAPAUDS sont des états d'âme, ils n'existent pas. Seuls
des étangs, des mélopées . . . L'enfant instruit de l'amertume
des bourgeons, l'enfant privé du lait obscur, casse comme le
verre. Une neige irréprochable récolte les sanglots, les éclats
d'une telle assomption lunaire. Et la machinerie hilare du
printemps s'affole, s'expatrie . . .

Accoutré des lambeaux d'un crime perpétré par des mains
étrangères sur un corps engourdi, tu progresses, tu déranges
les clartés et les signes, tu trembles dans l'éloge, tu meurs de
sécheresse aux abords de la pyramide. Dedans, ta pesanteur,
ton exégèse embaument. Le bonheur gronde, il fait nuit.

Il faut grandir avec douceur et démesure. Rajeunir les
gouffres, parquer les rois, s'enorgueillir. Les fenêtres sauvages
et les amours prostrées donnent sur un parfum.

LES FLEURS lorsqu'elles ne sont plus
leur fraîcheur gravit
d'autres montagnes d'air

et la volupté de respirer s'affine
entre les doigts qui tardent à se fermer

sur un outil impondérable

Là-bas c'est lui qui disparaît
sillon rapide, à l'aube, avant leur blessure
pour qu'elles s'ajoutent à d'autres liens,
fleurs, jusqu'à l'obscurité

lui, venu du froid et tourné vers le froid
comme toutes les routes qui surgissent . . .

O ash captivated under the tongue,
Gap in the horizon!

Between this star-packed rock and its sibling the abyss,
Breath's building is a second prison.

In place of the heart
You will touch, my love, only a glistening socket
And growing night . . .

The Palimpsest

TOADS ARE states of mind, they don't exist. Just ponds,
recitatives . . . The child who has learnt the bitterness of
buds, the child deprived of dark milk, breaks like glass. An
irreproachable snow harvests the sobs, the bursts of such a
lunar assumption. And the hilarious machinery of spring
panics, is exiled . . .

Accoutred in the shreds of a crime perpetrated by alien
hands on an insensate body, you progress, disturbing lights and
signs, trembling in praise, dying of dryness by the pyramid.
Inside, your weight, your exegesis embalm. Happiness growls,
it's night.

Growing must happen gently and immoderately. Re-
juvenating chasms, cooping up kings, getting proud. Untamed
windows and prostrate loves open on a perfume.

WHEN FLOWERS are dead
their coolness climbs
other hills of air

and the pleasure of breathing sharpens
between fingers that put off closing

on an impalpable instrument

Down there it's he that disappears
rapid furrow, at dawn, before their wounding
for them to add themselves to other links,
flowers, until darkness

he, come from the cold and facing the cold
like every road that meets him . . .

TANT QUE ma parole est obscure il respire

ses bras plongent dans l'eau glacée
entre les algues vers d'autres proies
glacées comme des lampes dans le jour

Si peu de réalité parvient au vivant
qu'il fasse violence ou qu'il sème
hardiment sur la pierre et les eaux

le ciel tendu la scansion des marteaux
quelques-uns parmi nous sont entrés intercédant
pour produire de nouveaux nuages

DANS LA chambre la nuit plonge
une lame fraîche et puissante
comme un aileron de requin

la nuit séparée des constellations

pendant que la montagne glisse
les racines du feu

                    portent à l'incandescence
la poussière du socle
et le sang
transpiré par le fer

MÊME SI de son cadavre
tout ce mâchefer est épris

sa mort a favorisé
l'élargissement d'une harpe de nerfs

la lenteur d'une épissure
aux prises avec les ongles
arrime le cri sous la bâche

j'invente le détour qui le rendrait vivant
et l'étendue du souffle
au-delà du harcèlement des limites

lattes rongées aspects du ciel

sporades d'un récit qui se perpétue
entre le ressac et la lie

As LONG as my speech is obscure he breathes

his arms plunge in freezing water
through the seaweed towards other prey
frozen as lamps in daylight

So little reality reaches the living man
whether he's brutal or sows
rashly on stone or water

sky stretched scansion of hammers
some of us have come interceding
to create new clouds

INTO THE room night plunges
a blade cool and strong
as a shark's fin

night parted from the constellations

while the mountain slips
the roots of fire

                fan to white-heat
the dust of the plinth
and blood
sweated out by steel

EVEN IF of his corpse
all this dross is enamoured

his death has permitted
a harp of nerves to open

the slowness of a splice
at odds with the fingernails
battens down the cry beneath the dragnet

I invent a detour to bring him alive
and the reach of breath
beyond the harassment of frontiers

corroded slats aspects of sky

seed-scatter of a narrative lasting
between eddy and dreg

JEAN JOUBERT
Trois poèmes immobiles

IV

ET NOUS vivrons sous le silence de la neige,
corps à corps, bouche à bouche, suspendus
dans le cristal d'invisibles feuillages.
Et les jours glisseront, les astres, les soleils,
jour après jour, nuit après nuit, et les années
s'amasseront en robes sombres à nos pieds.
Des arbres, des enfants naîtront de cette mort,
d'autres mains dénouées de l'herbe de nos mains,
des ailes bougeront entre nos bras déserts.
Nous verrons s'effacer, très loin sous nos fenêtres,
de petits gestes gris, des yeux bavards,
des ombres bues par de paisibles craies.
Nous les dirons de pluie, de feuilles, de passage,
rosée de sueur des terres maternelles,
ordre léger, poudre de nuit—si peu.
Dans le froid lumineux, nous survivons longtemps
à nos désirs—siècles, années, secondes—
sous le regard figé de l'oiseau blanc.

V

Le bourreau est maintenant cloué sur l'arbre,
la bête rouge, masquée de plumes,
dont l'oeil luisait comme tranchant de hache:
l'œil fendu, la main clouée
dans son vaste gant de corail.

Insecte dans la nuit d'écorce,
fourmi liquide, indifférente,
et, dans l'œil brusque des pies,
les couleurs confluentes de la mort.

Ma sœur, dis-moi ce qui désole ton visage.

Rien, rien, la paix du jour.

Déjà l'ennui sur l'eau tire ses linges.

Three Motionless Poems

IV

AND WE shall dwell beneath the hush of snow,
body to body, mouth to mouth, suspended
in the crystal of invisible boughs.
And the days will flicker past, the stars and suns,
day after day, night after night, the years
will mass in dark robes at our feet.
Trees and children will be born of this death,
other hands unloosed from the grass of our hands,
wings will stir between our desolate arms.
We shall see below our windows, far and small,
colourless gestures fading, garrulous eyes,
shadows consumed by the impassive chalk.
We shall call them the rain's, the leaves', transitory
dew of sweat of the maternal earth,
light in the scale, powder of night—a feather.
In the bright cold, we long outlive
our longings—centuries, years, seconds—
under the frozen stare of the white bird.

V

Now is the headsman nailed to the tree,
the scarlet brute, masked with plumes,
whose eyes gleamed like axe's cutting edge:
eye pierced, hand nailed
in its immense glove of coral.

Insect in the night of bark,
liquid ant, indifferent,
and in the sharp eyes of the magpie
the confluent tints of death.

Sister, tell me what saddens your gaze.

Nothing, nothing, the peace of day.

Already boredom draws its sheets across the water.

VII

Il a crié toute la nuit dans la clairière
ce cheval, abandonné par qui ? Bohémiens,
sorciers, soldats, voleurs de pierres,
sur cette terre où rien ne naît de rien.

Ou bien venu de sauvages frontières,
par les forêts, puisqu'il n'est pas lié,
que l'on ne voit ni selle ni lanière
dans l'aube où se délace la rosée.

Il me regarde. Une paupière tremble,
veinée de bleu. Sous les cils féminins,
son œil grandit, s'étoile, et il me semble
que le jour baisse aux rives des sapins.

Cheval de nuit cherchant un cavalier,
je ne t'attendais plus. La terre
déjà s'enflait. Les amandiers
avaient fleuri puis défleuri dans la lumière.

Mais cet appel dans l'aube des clairières,
et me voici contre ta robe, et nous irons,
laissant les jardins clos, vers le désert
où brûle au loin cet œil unique et rond.

JOYCE MANSOUR

CONNAIS-TU encore le doux arôme des plantaniers
Combien étranges peuvent être les choses familières après
  un départ
Combien triste la nourriture
Combien fade un lit
Et les chats
Te rappelles-tu les chats aux griffes stridentes
Qui hurlaient sur le toit quand ta langue me fouillait
Et qui faisaient le gros dos quand tes ongles m'écorchaient
Ils vibraient quand je cédais
Je ne sais plus aimer
Les bulles douloureuses du délire se sont évanouies de mes lèvres
J'ai abandonné mon masque de feuillage   *over*

VII

He has cried all night in the clearing,
this horse, abandoned by whom? Tinkers,
wizards, soldiery, quarry-thieves,
on this earth where nothing comes of nothing.

Or else he has escaped from savage frontiers
through the forests—for he isn't tethered,
and I see no thongs or saddle
in dawn's unlacing dew.

He watches me. An eyelid quivers,
blue-veined. Under feminine lashes
his eye dilates, fills with stars, and I see
daylight sinking over shores of pine.

Night-horse looking for a rider,
I never expected you again. Earth
was already bloated. The almonds
had flowered in the light, then overblown.

But this call in dawn's clearing,
And I am there touching your dress, and we shall leave
the walled garden, travel to the desert
where distant smoulders that one round eye.

DO YOU know the sweet smell of plantains
How strange familiar things can be after a departure
How depressing the food
How dreary a bed
And the cats
Do you remember the cats with caterwauling claws
Shrieking on the roof when your tongue explored me
Arching their backs when your nails clawed me
They vibrated when I yielded
I can't love any more
The painful bubbles of delirium have vanished from my lips
I have taken off my mask of leaves

Un rosier agonise sous le lit
Je ne me déhanche plus parmi la pierraille
Les chats ont déserté le toit

LA CHOUETTE bête des bois sombres
M'a appris
Que la vérité n'est plus la vérité
Sans ses voiles
Qu'il ne faut pas écouter la mélodie de la vie muette
Sans savoir l'entendre
Que la solitude modifie toutes les voix
Même celle de la haine
Que la lente douleur
Des paysans sans labeur
S'achète et se mange comme du pain
Que l'hostie souffre
Dans la féroce maladresse de l'appareil intestinal
Et surtout comment porter la fierté sur son dos
Sans avoir l'air
Bossu

CE N'EST pas de ma faute
Si mes cuisses sont moulées
Dans ma peau
Je n'ai pas voulu déclencher le rictus de ton désir
Quand j'ai retiré ma jupe
Garrotté de bonheur tu as saisi ma fente
Ce n'est pas de ma faute
Si l'alarme a sonné
Et ta main prise au piège
A été arrachée jugée bousculée
Et pendue par le cou telle une poupée de crème
Ce n'est pas de ma faute
Je voulais te pardonner

ON ÉCARTERA les cadavres
Le jour de ton départ
On pendra des coqs
Dans le creux des ogives
On boira le suc des années de souffrance
J'adopterai une fille

over

A rose-bush is dying under the bed
I no longer sway my hips among the stones
The cats have deserted the roof

THE SCREECH-OWL creature of the gloomy woods
Has taught me
That truth isn't truth any more
Without its veils
That you mustn't listen to the tune of mute life
Without knowing how to hear it
That loneliness alters all voices
Even the voice of hatred
That the unemployed peasants'
Slow sorrow
Is bought and eaten like bread
That the holy wafer suffers
In the savage clumsy apparatus of the bowels
And most of all how to carry pride on one's shoulders
Without looking
Hunchbacked

IT'S NOT my fault
If my thighs are shapely
In my skin
I didn't mean to spark off the rictus of your lust
When I took off my skirt
Strangled with delight you grabbed my slit
It's not my fault
If the alarm-bell rang
And your hand was trapped
Torn off sentenced hustled away
And hanged by the neck like a cream doll
It's not my fault
I meant to pardon you

WE'LL DRAG away the corpses
The day you go
We'll hang cockerels
In the arches' hollow
We'll drink the juice of years of suffering
I'll adopt a daughter

Un enfant
Un œuf de Pâques
Une vie
Et elle se souviendra
Du jour de ton départ
Car ton nom sera inscrit sur le damier de son esprit
En lettres majuscules de sang

JACQUES RÉDA
Mort d'un poète

ON LIT, dans une étude sur la poésie,
Que les poètes obsédés par la mort aujourd'hui
S'inspirent de la tradition germanique.
Cette remarque est une fleur séduisante de la culture,
Mais les sentiers de sa peur n'étaient pas fleuris,
Ils serpentaient autour d'une obscure caverne
Avec sa litière de fumier d'homme et d'os,
Et jamais nul soutien, nul appel ne lui vint
D'aucune tradition germanique ou autre, non,
Il travaillait sous la menace d'une primitive massue.
Ainsi *meurs* fut le sens brutal de la langue étrangère
Qu'il traduisit tant bien que mal dans le goût de l'époque,
Rêvant parfois qu'un dieu lettré, par égard pour cette agonie,
Etablirait son nom dans l'immortalité des livres.
Mais retenu du côté des sordides ancêtres,
Ignorant l'art du feu, dans la caverne il était seul
A savoir qu'il devait mourir de la même mort que les mots,
    les astres et les monstres.

Frontaliers

BÂTIS POUR abattre des arbres,
Tuer le porc ou broyer l'aviron,
Qui les a déroutés dès la lisière et faits lourds bûcherons
Dans la forêt d'allégorie où sont les bêtes véritables ?
Horlogers en hiver, quand la vieille âme hercynienne
Par la combe toujours humide et noire brame
Vers la neige jonchée encor de célestes lambeaux,
Quel coffre ils ont,
Défricheurs mais hantés par la maison détruite
Et, dans ce décombre nocturne, à l'abandon:

over

A child
An Easter-egg
A life
And she'll remember
The day you went
For your name shall be engraved upon the chessboard of her soul
In capital letters of blood

Death of a Poet

I READ, in a study on poetry,
That today's poets obsessed by death
Are inspired by the Germanic tradition.
This remark is one of culture's seductive blooms,
But the lanes of his fear were not floral,
They enlaced a dark cavern
With its bedding of human dung and bones,
And no support, no appeal ever reached him
From a Germanic tradition or any other, no,
He laboured in the shadow of a primitive club.
So *die* was the brutal meaning of that foreign tongue
He struggled to translate for contemporary taste,
Sometimes dreaming that a literate god, respecting his anguish,
Would establish his name in the immortality of books.
But held back among our squalid ancestors,
Not knowing the art of fire, he alone in the cave
Knew he must die the same death as words, stars and
    monsters.

Frontiersmen

BUILT FOR felling trees,
Sticking a pig or snapping an oar,
Who at the margin misdirected them and made them
    tough woodcutters
In the forest of allegory, home of the real wild beasts?
Watchmakers in winter, when the old Hercynian spirit
Bells through the damp black glen
Towards snow still strewn with tatters of sky,
Barrel-chested,
Pioneers but haunted by destruction of their homes
Defenceless in the wreckage of night:

Des petits au cul nu dont les mains ne seront plus jointes
Après la soupe, et comme il faisait bon;
Coffre d'os et de grosses bronches qui raclent
Entre la salamandre et le hibou, la hache
Vibrant en la faille de chair du rien qui parle.

Personnages dans la banlieue

VOUS N'EN finissez pas d'ajouter encore des choses,
Des boîtes, des maisons, des mots.
Sans bruit l'encombrement s'accroît au centre de la vie,
Et vous êtes poussés vers la périphérie,
Vers les dépotoirs, les autoroutes, les orties;
Vous n'existez plus qu'à l'état de débris ou de fumée.
Cependant vous marchez,
Donnant la main à vos enfants hallucinés
Sous le ciel vaste, et vous n'avancez pas;
Vous piétinez sans fin devant le mur de l'étendue
Où les boîtes, les mots cassés, les maisons vous rejoignent,
Vous repoussent un peu plus loin dans cette lumière
Qui a de plus en plus de peine à vous rêver.
Avant de disparaître,
Vous vous retournez pour sourire à votre femme attardée,
Mais elle est prise aussi dans un remous de solitude,
Et ses traits flous sont ceux d'une vieille photographie.
Elle ne répond pas, lourde et navrante avec le poids du jour
    sur ses paupières,
Avec ce poids vivant qui bouge dans sa chair et qui
    l'encombre,
Et le dernier billet du mois plié dans son corsage.

Matin d'octobre

LEV DAVIDOVITCH BRONSTEIN agite sa barbiche, agite
Ses mains, sa chevelure hirsute; encore un peu, il va
Bondir de son gilet et perdre ses besicles d'érudit,
Lui qui parle aux marins de Cronstadt taillés dans le bois mal
Equarri de Finlande, et guère moins sensibles que
Les crosses des fusils qui font gicler la neige sale.
Il prêche, Lev Davidovitch, il s'époumone, alors
Que sur le plomb de la Néva lentement les tourelles
Du croiseur *Aurora* vers la façade obscure du   *over*

Little bare-bummed kids who'll never link hands again
After soup, and how good it was;
Hooped with bone and thick bronchi rasping
Between lizard and owl, the axe quivering
In the flesh-seam of what is nothing, but speaks.

Characters in the Suburbs

YOU KEEP on piling up more and more objects,
Boxes, houses, words.
Silently congestion grows in the centre of living,
And you are pushed towards the outskirts,
Towards cesspools, motorways, nettles;
You no longer exist but as rubbish or smoke.
Meanwhile you walk
Hand in hand with your moonstruck children
Under the empty sky, getting nowhere;
You tramp on and on beside immensity's fence
Where boxes, broken words and houses meet you,
Push you a little further out into the light
That finds it harder and harder to dream you.
Before disappearing,
You turn round to smile at your dallying wife,
But she's caught too in an eddy of solitude,
Features blurred like an old snapshot.
She doesn't answer, harrowing and heavy, daylight
    weighing on her eyelids,
The living weight stirring in her body, encumbering her,
And the month's last banknote folded in her blouse.

October Morning

LEV DAVIDOVICH BRONSTEIN wags his goatee, waves
His hands, his bushy hair; you'd think he would
Pop from his waistcoat and drop his professorial spectacles,
As he talks to the Kronstadt sailors carved in the rough
Hewn wood of Finland, and barely less tender than
The riflebutts spattering dirty snow.
Lev Davidovich is preaching, bawling his lungs out, whilst
On the lead of the Neva slowly the turrets
Of the cruiser *Aurora* level on the Winter Palace's

Palais d'Hiver se tournent.

        Quel bagou; quel ciel jaune;
Quel poids d'histoire sur les ponts déserts où parfois ronfle
Une voiture aux ailes hérissées de baïonnettes.
A Smolny, cette nuit, les barbes ont poussé; les yeux,
Brûlés par le tabac et le filament des ampoules,
Chavirent, Petrograd, devant ton crépuscule, ton silence
Où là-bas, au milieu des Lettons appliqués et farouches,
Lev Davidovitch prophétise, exhorte, menace, tremble
Aussi de sentir la masse immobile des siècles
Basculer sans retour, comme les canons sur leur axe,
Au bord de ce matin d'octobre.

        (Et déjà Vladimir
Ilitch en secret a rejoint la capitale; il dormira
Plus tard, également grimé, dans un cercueil de verre,
Immobile toujours sous les bouquets et les fanfares.
Cependant Lev Davidovitch agite sa tignasse,
Rattrape son lorgnon,

        —un peu de sang, un peu de ciel
Mexicain s'y mélangeront le dernier jour, si loin
De toi boueux octobre délirant au vent des drapeaux rouges.)

Septembre

CE QUI se lève tout à coup dans la lumière, annonçant
   l'automne;
Et ce vent des jours oubliés flottant comme une pèlerine;
Et ces arbres appareillant non vers la neige ou les brouillards
   déjà sous les collines,
Mais vers la mer intérieure où le ciel se déploie
Et dans un ciel plus haut comme un drapeau fragile se
   déchire,
Arbres rentrant au port enfin, feux rallumés en autrefois.
(Autrefois reste la patrie.
Et de nouveau septembre ici
Ramène la halte du ciel et des arbres d'automne
En vain: nous ne reviendrons pas,
Bien que cette clarté se lève encore sur les bois
Et submerge les prés où nos pas ne couchent plus l'herbe
Ayant ce peu de poids des morts et de leur nostalgie.)

Dim façade.
                    What a gift of the gab; what a bright yellow sky;
What a weight of history loading the empty bridges where
    sometimes a car
Wings bristling with bayonets goes snorting by.
At Smolny last night, beards grew; eyes,
Smarting with tobacco and the filaments of lamps,
Roll, Petrograd, before your half-light, your silence
Where among fierce and earnest Letts
Lev Davidovich prophesies, urges, threatens, trembles too
Feeling the motionless mass of centuries
Irrevocably tipping like the guns on their axes
On the edge of this October morning.
                              (And already Vladimir
Ilyich has reached the capital incognito; he'll sleep
Later, smoothly made-up, in a glass coffin,
Motionless for ever under wreaths and fanfares.
Meanwhile Lev Davidovich wags his mop of hair,
Catches his specs
              —a little blood, a little
Mexican sky will mingle with them on the last day, so far
From you, muddy October, wild in the wind of red flags.)

September

A SUDDEN difference in the light, announcing autumn;
And this wind from forgotten days flapping like a cape;
And these trees setting sail not for snow or the mist
    already fringing the hills,
But to the inland sea where sky unfurling
Into deeper sky, rips like a threadbare flag,
Trees reaching harbour at last, beacons lit in yesterday.
(Yesterday is still home.
And here September again
Calls sky and autumn trees to a standstill
In vain: we'll not return,
Although this brightness still rises on the woods
And drowns the meadows where our steps no longer
    flattening the grass
Weigh as little as the dead, as the dead's nostalgia.)

Soir

COMME NOUS voici loin du clapotis bleu des collines
Qui bat contre les murs que va démanteler le soir;
Ici; ne bougeons pas; le souvenir de cet instant
Qui vient se penche sur nos fronts et nous sommes perdus,
Bien qu'une branche rame encore et cherche à nous sortir
Du remous désormais figé qui nous retient.
                                        Si près
Qu'on y pourrait tremper la main, la source s'abandonne
Au bonheur précaire du temps qui coule, mais nos voix
Semblent demander l'heure, encore incrédules: déjà
Leur écho s'est éteint parmi les arbres immobiles.
Nous voici là, debout dans la lumière de l'exil,
Interrogeant en vain notre ombre au soleil qui décroît.

La terre qui s'éloigne

NOUS POUVONS dire *ici*,
Douces briques sans fin recuites par le désert,
Furent Ninive et Babylone; mais la terre,
Quand elle aura comme un charbon sanglant dispersé dans
   le ciel
Nos os, nos codes et le soc des dernières charrues,
Qui dira, désignant cet orbe annulé dans l'espace,
Ici fut le nid appendu entre les branches du soleil,
Le feuillage de l'arbre de parole et sa racine
Arrachée et jetée au feu sans flamme de l'éther?
(Et déjà nous nous éloignons un peu dans le sifflement des
   fusées;
Du sas étroit, l'éclaireur des routes d'étoiles
Emerge, et de ses bras épais saisit la terre mère
Comme la tête d'un enfant perdu qui reparaît en songe—
Et nul n'a plus de voix, ni le rêve, ni le dormeur,
Ni la nuit véhémente qui les emporte.)

Amen

NUL SEIGNEUR je n'appelle, et pas de clarté dans la nuit.
La mort qu'il me faudra contre moi, dans ma chair, prendre
   comme une femme,
Est la pierre d'humilité que je dois toucher en esprit,
Le degré le plus bas, la séparation intolérable

Evening

HOW FAR are we now from the hills' blue lapping
Lapping against the walls that evening will dismantle;
Here; don't move; the memory of this coming
Moment leans over our foreheads and we are lost,
Though a branch still sculls seeking to rescue us
From the whirlpool's grip now freezing.
                                        So close
We could dip our hands in, the spring surrenders
To the precarious joy of flowing time, but our voices
Seem to ask the hour, still incredulous: already
Their echo has died among the motionless trees.
Here we are, standing in the light of exile,
Vainly questioning our shadows in the declining sun.

Receding Earth

WE CAN say *here*,
Soft bricks endlessly rebaked by the desert,
Were Nineveh and Babylon; but when earth
Like a blood-hot coal has scattered in the sky
Our bones, our codes and the last ploughshares,
Who will say, pointing out this orb annulled in space,
Here was the nest hung in the sun's branches,
The leaves of the tree of speech and its root
Torn out and cast on ether's flameless fire ?
(And already we're a step further off in the whistle of
    rockets;
Through fate's tight airlock, the scout of the star-roads
Emerges, his clumsy arms seize mother earth
Like the head of a lost child seen in a dream—
And nothing has voice any longer, dream or sleeper,
Or headlong night as it carries them away.)

Amen

NO LORD I name, and see no light in the darkness.
Death that I must, close to me, into my body, take
    like a woman,
Is the stone of humility I must touch in spirit,
The bottommost step, the unbearable parting

D'avec ce que je saisirai, terre ou main, dans l'abandon
   sans exemple de ce passage—
Et ce total renversement du ciel qu'on n'imagine pas.
Mais qu'il soit dit ici que j'accepte et ne demande rien
Pour prix d'une soumission qui porte en soi la récompense.
Et laquelle, et pourquoi, je ne sais point:
Où je m'agenouille il n'est ni foi ni orgueil, ni espérance,
Mais comme à travers l'œil qu'ouvre la lune sous la nuit,
Retour au paysage impalpable des origines,
Cendre embrassant la cendre et vent calme qui la bénit.

JEAN-PIERRE DUPREY
6e Nuit

AUX AYANTS droit, donnez
Le bonjour de Sainte Anne.
Aux ayants donné, prenez
Ce qui ne reste pas.

Et toi, le reste:
—Matelasse tes hannetons,
Briquette ton mur,
Vide ton creux.
Dépense ton toit en quatre sous d'ardoise
Et pense la nuit par son grand trou.

Mouvement

MOUVEMENT PLIÉ au corps de la vie
Dehors, la nuit neigée à l'étendue
Dedans, le mort qui n'attend plus
Qu'un seul battement d'aile
Dont l'endroit
Est encore ombre de l'envers.

Et cet endroit est cet envers
Passé à travers cet endroit.

Mouvement sans poids sur les mains
Dont le dos
S'applique aux vitres sans mesure.
Lentement, peinant de quatre membres d'air,
D'air engourdi,

over

From what I shall grasp, earth or hand, in the
  incomparable abandon of that passing—
And the sky capsizing, not to be imagined.
But let me say at once that I accept and ask for nothing
As price of a submission carrying its own reward.
And what reward, and why, I do not know:
Where I kneel there is neither faith nor pride, nor hope,
But as through the moon's eye opened in night,
Return to the intangible country of origins,
Ash embracing ash and calm wind blessing it.

6th Night

TO THOSE who've rights, give
St Anne's good-day.
To those who've given, take
What isn't left.

And you, the rest:
Pack up your bats,
Brick up your wall,
Pour out your vacuum.
Spend your roof on four ha'pence of tile
And think night through its great hole.

Movement

MOVEMENT IN line with life's body
Outside, night snowing up space
Inside, a dead man waiting for just
One wing-beat
Whose whereabouts
Is still a shadow of nowhere.

And this whereabouts is this nowhere
Inserted in this whereabouts.

Movement not weighing on the hands
Whose back
Leans against measureless windows.
Slowly, with four straining limbs of air,
Numbed air,

Passé comme à la lenteur des murs,
Le mort appuie l'ouvert de sa tête.

Chanson à reculons

MONTÉ DARE-DARE sur mon cheval Pied,
Moi qui né pour, qui n'est point, qui n'est plus
Qu'une épine que j'existe
Dans son propre pied,
J'ai pour une main cinq gallons,
Dans le temps j'ai un: Allons!
J'ai à la tête un encerclant,
Enserre quand et qui et quoi et clou,
J'ai dans la bouche un trou
Cerné de clous.

Mais qu'est-ce que ça?
Mais qui
Mais qui s'en va-t-à? . . .
Voici venir l'Etre qui va
Sur l'air de n'être pas.

Et des dents et des dents, dedans
J'ai.
Ma tête dans la bouche ne fera pas,
Ne ferme pas ce qu'est affaire de mort,
Comme font les mots de rien
Comme de tout, comme du tout,
N'est pas du tout totalitaire.

Mais qui,
Mais qui s'en va-t-à? . . .
Le tout sur l'air de pas . . .

C'est ici, l'air roulé à point,
A pas, à plus, à moins qu'une boule,
C'est ici l'air de quoi?
Mais qu'est-ce que ça?—qui n'est pas plus—,
Mais qui,
Mais qui s'en va-t-à? . . .
Voici venir l'Etre qui va
Sur l'air de n'être pas.
Et pour un autre et batterie baptisée Corps
Voici la manivelle Etcétéra . . .

Passing at the slowness of walls,
The dead man's head presses on the outwhere.

Song Sung Backwards

RIDE-A-COCK-HORSE on my charger Foot,
I who was born for, borne off, am bare
Ly a thorn that I exist
In its own foot, I've
For a hand got five
Bars, in time I've a: Letsbeoff!
Round my crown I've a bound
Wound round when and who and titfer tack
In my mouth I've a hole
Rimmed with tin-tacks.

But what is that?
And who
Whoever's off to . . .?
Here comes a man who goes no where
On no-man's air.

And fangs upon fangs, pangs I'd
Inside.
My head in my mouth won't do,
Won't shut down dead on what to-do with death,
As words for nothing do
For anything at all
'S not at all-in-all.

But who,
Whoever's off to . . .?
And all on an air of no . . .

It's where? It's here, it's air spun down to a dot,
To a not, to a nor, to a smaller than a ball,
It's here an air of what?
But what can it be?—that's barely more—
And who,
Whoever's off to . . .?
Here comes a man who goes no where
On no-man's air.
And for some-body else and battery baptized Body
Here comes the Etcetera-handle . . .

JEAN BRETON
Dans la poche

J'AVAIS FAIM de tes jambes, double bond de pain chaud.
Au deuxième rendez-vous, ce fut *dans la poche*.

Quelle force t'a renversée, au ralenti,
sur ce couvre-lit anonyme ?
Des tiges d'eau confessent une origine.
Ton chignon de mousse chancelle.

Ta gaine trop serrée t'empêchait de respirer,
coquette ! N'invente pas l'excuse des bas.
J'ai dû compter quatorze baisers
et le naufrage du soutien-gorge avant l'abandon.

A moi, tes dents, comme un os de rosée !
A moi, tes yeux, fente sur l'invisible !
Quand ta main m'appelle pour la première fois,
j'ai envie de tutoyer Dieu comme un frère.

Le lit tangue de joie et de surprise.
Des fleurs sont écrasées
sur le seuil de la cabane d'urine
abri de qui naîtra
cette fois sans connaître sa mort.

A Casablanca, l'homme en blanc
place des pinces sur ton ventre
dans la lumière bouton d'or
où tournent des miettes de sang.

CLAUDE MICHEL CLUNY
Le bal à la mer

PRENEZ VOS masques, vos couronnes, vos amantes. La mer
approche, et dresse ses remparts écroulés sur une foule en
perruque blanche. Le phare bat par à-coups ; le bal s'allume en
costume de sel ; on n'entend pas les astres frissonner dans
l'eau des mares, mais claquer au vent tout un ciel humide.
Voiles de seins naufragés, des robes d'écume se gonflent et
retombent en gerbes . . . Masqueé, la nuit s'avance dans
l'eau des ports, entre les lustres. Alors, le crabe sort son trapèze
étrange. Chacun reconnaît Louis XV ; il ouvre le bal au bras
des ténèbres.

In the Bag

I WAS hungry for your legs, twin leap of warm bread.
At the second meeting, it was *in the bag*.

What force threw you in slow motion
on that anonymous bedspread?
Stems of water confess an origin.
Your moss chignon topples.

Your corset was too tight for you to breathe,
coquette! Don't invent the excuse of stockings.
I must have counted fourteen kisses
and the shipwreck of your bra before surrender.

Mine, your teeth, like a bone of dew!
Mine, your eyes, peephole on the invisible!
When your hand calls me for the first time,
I feel like calling God my brother.

The bed tilts with joy and surprise.
Flowers are crushed
on the threshold of the latrine
shelter of someone who'll be born
this time without knowing his death.

At Casablanca, the man in white
rests the forceps on your stomach
in the buttercup light
aswim with crumbs of blood.

The Sea Dance

TAKE UP your masks, your crowns, your mistresses. The sea
approaches, and builds its crumbling ramparts over a white-
wigged crowd. The lighthouse pulses; the ball lights up in a salt
dress; you hear, not the stars shivering in their pools, but a big
wet sky flapping in the wind. Sails of shipwrecked breasts,
skirts of foam billow and drop in showers . . . Masked, night
closes in over harbour waters, between the chandeliers. Then
the crab scuttles out his strange trapezoid. Everyone recog-
nizes Louis XV; he opens the dance on the arm of darkness.

Egée

LES DALLES de marbre de l'île
sont couleur de l'été. Partout
une flamme courte qui bouge.

L'air aux yeux d'émail se penche sur un pêcheur
et va l'aimer.

Les cigales cisèlent
la statue bleue du jour.

Je pense à cet amour à l'air si jeune et grave
   —et moi en moi seul je voyage . . .
Mon ombre est passée de l'autre côté de moi
Comme un noyé s'avance
   vers l'autre face de la mer.

Racines

MON VISAGE en attente
près de tes bras aveugles
me regarde descendre
en toi, terre profonde
lit sans désir où je serai si calme
moi que rien rien jamais ne garde

Amour ma chair s'attarde
moment dernier du jour.

Il faut que je me hâte
et descende en ce jardin connu de toi seul . . .
Pourrissant en merveilles
je serai ce petit arbre pour ton été,
où dort une guitare au chiffre de septembre.

Que l'odeur de la terre s'élève de moi,
et celle de la nuit mouillée de sève.
Et du secret noué de mes racines,
le silence éloge de l'ombre.

Pelouse

VOUS DEVRIEZ savoir que je laisse toujours mes yeux dans
les arbres, attentifs sur les tiges de la menthe, ou dans la verte
lumière du thé   *over*

Aegean

THE ISLAND'S marble flags
are the colour of summer. Everywhere
a brief flame moving.

Enamel-eyed air leans over a fisherman
lovingly.

The cicadas chisel away
at day's blue statue.

I think of this love with its young grave air
　　—and I voyage only in myself . . .
My shadow has passed to the other side of me
Like a drowned man moving
　　　to the sea's other surface.

Roots

MY FACE waiting
by your blind arms
watches me descend
into you, deep earth
bed without desire where I shall lie so still
I whom nothing nothing ever retains

Love my body loiters
day's last moment.

I must hurry
to go down into this garden known by you alone . . .
Rotting into miracles
I shall be a little tree in your summer
where a guitar sleeps at September's cypher.

Let the smell of the earth rise from me,
and that of the sap-wet night.
And from the knotted secret of my roots,
silence, the eulogy of shadow.

Lawn

YOU SHOULD know I always leave my eyes in the trees,
watchful on sprigs of mint, or in the tea-green light

et cela me gêne un peu quand je vais à la ville mais c'est vous que je veux voir rêvant sempiternelle sur votre pelouse grand lit d'asphodèles et de fleurs du chili qu'épient le soir les naissantes étoiles du lynx

mais pas un geste, à peine si vous laissez paraître que vos seins s'ennuient et je n'ai d'autre recours qu'errer sans voix et sans visage mes yeux à chat perché dans les nuages ou sur la haie redoutable du houx

alors que mon corps s'en va vers la ville et ses vains travaux, le bûcher des livres, l'écroulement des remparts et l'irrésistible montée des eaux dont le flot emporte les navires entre mes lèvres étonnées, sans le dire !

FERNAND OUELLETTE
Parce que femelle

DE DÉFAILLANCE en défaillance en toi me désagrège
plus acéré que ta nudité,
dissipant ma musique et sa magie, toujours
plus tenaillé par l'inapaisable.
Et cette soif de l'entaille que tu n'as pu guérir
de la courbe que tu n'as pas conçue.

Provocante mais si saine parce que bien femelle
je t'irrite en devenant ton idolâtre ton mage
devenu ta chose.

Et ces torsions qui tiennent à l'outre-terre,
à quelque gouffre d'où je reviens inextinguible.
Mais tu fuis mes sondes à feu, mes débâcles
de fleuve sensitif.
Tu repousses parfois mes lubies bien au noir,
comme des bijoux brisés que tu laisses au . . .

Et pourtant tu es mon projet en haut de la flamme,
ma charnelle où germe l'aube,
et pourtant tu es la pierre
où ne s'use mon mal de sens.

Totem antéhumain

MON TOTEM
ma femme héraldique bien enfouie.   *over*

and this hampers me somewhat when I go into town but it's
you I want to see dreaming sempiternal on your lawn great
bed of asphodels and chilean flowers spied on at evening by
the opening stars of the lynx

   but not a gesture, you barely reveal how bored your breasts
are and all I can do is wander on voiceless and faceless my
eyes cat-crouched in the clouds or on the holly's forbidding
hedge

   whilst my body travels off to the town and its aimless acti-
vity, the pyre of books, the ramparts crumbling, the waters
irresistibly rising, washing away the ships between my
amazed lips, not saying so!

Because Female

FROM FAINTING to fainting in you I disintegrate
sharper than your nakedness,
dispelling my music and its magic, always
more tortured by the unappeasable.
And this thirst for the wound that you have not cured
for the curve you have not conceived.

Provocative but so whole because so female
I offend you becoming your idolater your magician
become your thing.

And these torsions belonging to the other-world,
to some chasm from which I return inextinguishable.
But you evade my fire-plummets, the defeats
of my visionary river.
Sometimes you push my fancies out into darkness,
like broken toys that you leave to the . . .

And yet you are my flame-tip purpose,
my carnal woman where dawn seeds,
and yet you are the whetstone
where my sense-ache never wears out.

Prehuman Totem

MY TOTEM
my deep-buried heraldic woman.

Attentif je l'ai retirée de ma tourbe,
suspendue sur un cintre beau vermillon.
Il suffit parfois de la dépendre sous
le coup d'un élancement plus dur.

Certes la belle étoffe s'est fort refroidie,
et même amplifiée comme une morte naissant
de l'onde voisine de la morte Aphrodite.

Mais quelle image, quelle grande dame
se laisse encor partager
quelle fragile s'accoutume aux séismes
du froid profanateur
du fol adorateur ?

Réveil

DE CHAIR je sortis souffrant comme
un nageur quitte la mer blanche.
Je pris la forêt en feuilles pour
ratisser le froid en poussière
dans ma brûlance.
Lorsque je touchai au bleu
qui sur l'arbre s'écorchait :
il me cracha sur l'âme.

Naufrage

IMMOBILE MAIS balisée par des odeurs,
cherchant la proie jusqu'à l'ange :
elle s'étendit sur le drap froid
parfaitement fleuve parsemé de joncs fauves.

Dans un éclair ma vie s'y déposa,
vif corbeau dans la moisson dolente.

Ainsi se laissa-t-elle assaillir et dévaster
sous les cris des mains
et polir par la langue dans les ombrages.

Quand sur le flanc elle revint,
comme une amphore de la flamme,
sa peau était ici et là moirée et mauve
de pensées naufragées en profondeur.

Assiduous I drew her from my peat,
hung her on a fine vermilion arch.
Sufficient sometimes to take her down
under the thrust of a harder urge.

To be sure the fine material has grown cold,
and even amplified like a dead woman born
from the wave beside dead Aphrodite.

But what image, what great lady
still lets herself be shared
what fragile woman adjusts to the earth-tremor
of the cold profaner
of the frenzied worshipper?

Awakening

I LEFT the body suffering like
a swimmer leaving the white sea.
I took the forest in leaf to
rake the cold in dust
in my burning.
When I touched the blue
grazed by the tree,
it spat on my soul.

Shipwreck

MOTIONLESS BUT beaconed by odours,
hunting her prey even to the angel:
she stretched out on the cold sheet
perfectly river strewn with tawny rushes.

In a flash my life settled there,
quick crow in the grieving harvest.

Thus she let herself be assailed and ravaged
under the shout of hands
and polished in her shadows by the tongue.

When on her side she returned,
like an amphora from the flame,
her skin was here and there moired and mauve
with deepsea shipwrecked thoughts.

Le lit

QUEL LIT profond ! où je passais de l'ange
à la sueur.
Ma bouche te révélait le torse,
plénitude, mue de toi,
furieusement vers la blessure immuable
et première,
qui nous frappe à jamais de mort blanche.

Et mes lèvres cueillaient ton âme sous tes seins,
dans l'énigme de la parole brune
sur flanelle.
Au loin ta chevelure si répandue
comme un rêve,
à peine humaine,
accrochait des lumières peut-être solaires
peut-être infernales
d'où cillaient les signes de notre extase.

Alignements

CONTRE LE funéraire
                                        je brûle !
Le long des alignements de membres
de fleurs se donnant au noir.
Qui soutient ce silence stérile ?

Le beau dolmen des tourterelles
(ah croît le filet du minéral)
les assonances des odeurs
                                        terrassantes
les aimants de puissantes chaleurs :
mais tout se ferme au grand culte !

L'âge d'or de ton corps
qui s'en souviendra ?
si tu déclines par le fané la dispersion
loin des anciens éclats du gui.

The Bed

SO DEEP a bed! where I passed from angel
to sweat.
My mouth revealed your body to you,
fulness, moved by you,
furiously towards the immutable
primal wound,
that strikes us for ever with white death.

And my lips plucked the soul from beneath your breasts,
in the mystery of the brown word
on flannel.
Far off your hair so spread
like a dream,
barely human,
caught lights perhaps solar
perhaps infernal
where the zodiac signs of our ecstasy flickered.

Alignments

AGAINST THE funereal
                              I burn!
Along alignments of limbs
of flowers yielding to darkness.
Who sustains this arid silence?

The beautiful dolmen of doves
(O the mineral kingdom spreading its net)
the assonating scents
                              exhausting,
magnets of violent heats:
but everything closes on the great rite!

Your body's golden age
who will remember it?
if you decline by fading, scattered
far from the bursts of ancient mistletoe.

MICHEL DEGUY
Le golfe

LE LONG été commence où croît et décroît l'ambition
Je vis au niveau des éruptions stridentes des sauterelles
Et parmi les insectes de papier que disperse le vent
Il y a du seigle sur les genoux de l'écrivain et dans son
  dos pleuvent les blés
L'oreille appliquée à la terre entend son sang
Il est le désœuvré

La roue du paysage tourne sous le triomphe du soleil
Les raies blanches du ciel convergent au-delà de la terre
Les îles s'effilochent, la marée décèle des ruches d'algues
  couleurs de débris
Où fermentent des invertébrés
Vois toute la rotation horizontale du golfe,
Le glissement des bocages, le grincement des bornages de genêt,
Rayons verts sur le moyeu de l'horizon !

Si je reprends les chemins profonds — faut-il encore s'en
  entretenir ?
Je vais lentement aux rendez-vous essentiels
Le vent traverse la presqu'île pliant les blés vers l'Est
Partout la mer m'assaille car le vent du large lui ouvre
  passage entre les haies
Entre les orges entre les châtaigniers
L'Océan épais monte entre les toits

Le vent rapide descend les trois hauts degrés des pins, des
  genêts et des blés
Il se rue frôlant les oreilles et passe
Le soleil à reculons fait face Le soleil acrobate descend du
  chapiteau
Interminable
Parfois des spectateurs repèrent l'exercice Mais beaucoup
  l'été se couchent avant la fin

Le vent parle trop fort
Dans les trous du vent se glissent les chiens des fermes éloignées
L'alouette ne cesse de tomber Le vent se fraie un passage
  jusqu'aux premiers rangs des champs   *over*

The Gulf

LONG SUMMER starts where ambition wanes and waxes
I live down among the shrill outbursts of grasshoppers
Among paper insects scattered by the wind
There's rye on the writer's knees and a rain of corn
     on his back
Ear to the ground hearing the blood
No work on his hands

In a triumph of sunlight the wheel of landscape turns
Out beyond land, the sky's white bands converge
Islands fray away, the tide uncovers honeycombs of
     debris-coloured seaweed
A ferment of bivalves
See how the gulf horizontally rotates,
Its copses blurring, its squeaking landmarks of broom,
Green spokes on the horizon's hub!

If I walk the sunken lanes—need it be mentioned
     again?—
slowly I go to the primal meeting-place
The wind blows over the headland bending the corn
     eastwards
On all sides assailed by sea for the deepsea wind opens it
     a path through the hedges
Through the barley through the chestnuts
Solid Ocean rises between the roofs

The wind leaps down three high steps of pines, broom
     and corn
Whisks past my ears and away
Doggèd, the sun backs off The acrobat sun swarms down
     from its capital
Interminably
Sometimes spectators watch out this exercize But many
     in summer go to bed before it's over

The wind speaks out too loud
Into holes in the wind sneak dogs from distant farms
The lark keeps endlessly falling The wind cuts its way
     to the fields' front line

Il enjambe violemment la lisière de paille et se jette aux oreilles

Des chiens gardent des chemins sans importance d'où je suis
Les voix qui miment les bêtes pour leur commander
Issues des niches plus hautes où elles veillent sur les biens
Passent par les trous du vent
Hélant pour des travaux sans importance d'où je suis

Promenades en vue de quoi ?
Le corbeau sans couleur
La mouette qui arrête le vent
La lune, cirrus obèse, qui marque où le vent ne souffle plus

Car il manque aux pas la constance du vent
Du vent qui sait aux papillons aux fougères aux nuages
Indiquer la direction
Orienter insistant courber repassant diriger rassembler dans
    son souffle incliner joindre
—et tout à coup redresser cabrer recourber tordre
Le vent parcourt le site, ajointe et fait communiquer les
    lignes du site
Lui de haut de partout les suit
C'est lui qui trace les sillons du site

Tout en moi répond au vent—sauf . . .
Tout plie sous l'injonction qui assemble :
les cheveux comme un champ plus dense
le dos pareil aux troncs, les yeux dessillés sous le sel
les jambes écroulées dans les pierres
Et la manducation au bruit de charrette ; tout . . .
Sauf la voix debout qui demande où elle naît ; tout
Sauf la voix étonnée de sa dissemblance !

Le grand vaisseau du matin appareille :
Cris de poulies des mouettes ; cordages du soleil dans les yeux ;
    hautes trinquettes des cumulus hissées brassées drossées ;
    un équipage d'alouettes qui survole les basses vergues des
    frênes ; les corbeaux quartiers-maîtres
Et le grand spinaker de l'orage . . .

Fiercely jumps the straw verge and hurls itself at hearing

Dogs guard the routeless lanes I come from
Voices that imitate cattle to control them
Voices from higher kennels watching over property
Pass through holes in the wind
Hallooing for toil to me idle

What is this walking for?
The colourless crow
The gull that checks the wind
The moon, fat cirrhus, marking where the wind no longer blows

For steps lack the wind's insistency
The wind that to butterflies bracken and clouds
Shows the way
Steers steadily snatches flattens bows unites
—lifts suddenly tosses rears bends fro and twines
The wind sweeps over the site, conjoins and links its lines
Surveys its every point from aloft
Traces its furrows

Everything in me responds to the wind—except . . .
Everything bends to its gathering command:
hair like a denser field
back like a tree-trunk, eyes unsealed to the salt
legs toppled among stones
And the crunching of a cart; everything . . .
Except the voice upright, demanding its source; everything
Except the voice amazed at its own unlikeness!

Morning's tall ship is setting sail:
Gulls squeak like pulleys; the sun's cordage glints in the eyes;
    high staysails of cumulus hoisted braced and driven; a crew
    of larks flying over ash-tree yardarms; the quartermaster
    crows
And the storm's great spinaker . . .

LES JOURS ne sont pas comptés
Sachons former un convoi de déportés qui chantent
Arbres à flancs de prières
Ophélie au flottage du temps
Assonances guidant un sens vers le lit du poème

Comment appellerons-nous ce qui donne le ton ?
La poésie comme l'amour risque tout sur des signes

ALLUVION DES cris Minerai d'hirondelles
Dans le delta du vent les plissements du vent
    La trembleraie bleuit
Le pouls de l'étang bat
    Toutes les trois heures un poème
    Devient nouveau puis se ternit
    Sous la lecture Recroît dans le silence

QUAI GRIS d'où tombe l'appât de neige
Le jour décline dans sa coïncidence
L'homme et la femme échangent leur visage
Le vin est lent sur le tableau
A passer dans son sablier de verre
Et l'artiste rapide au cœur par symboles
Doué de confiance hésite :
La pierre est-elle plus belle dans le mur ?

MORAINE BLEUE dans le glacier du soir

La vigne rentre sous le vert, le bleu reprend le
ciel, le sol s'efface dans la terre, le rouge
s'exhausse et absorbe en lui les champs de Crau.
Les couleurs s'affranchissent des choses et
retrouvent leur règne épais et libre avant
les choses, pareilles à la glaise qui précédait Adam

Le saurien terre émerge et lève mâchoire
vers la lune, les années rêveuses sortent des grottes
et rôdent tendrement autour de la peau épaisse Falaise se
redresse, Victoire reprend son âge pour la nuit. Les nuages
même s'écartent, les laissant.

    En hâte quittée cette terre qui tremble
ils se sont regroupés dans la ville, bardés de portes.

THE DAYS aren't counted
Let's form a convoy of deportees singing
Trees with a bark of prayers
Ophelia rafted on time
Assonance guiding sense to the poem's bed

How shall we name what gives the tone?
Poetry like love risks all on signs

ALLUVIUM OF cries Ore of swallows
In the wind's delta the wind's creases
    The aspen-grove turns blue
The pond's pulse beats
    Every three hours a poem
    Becomes new then tarnishes
    In the reading Grows again in silence

GREY JETTY where the bait of snow is falling
The day declines into coincidence
Man and woman exchange faces
The wine is slow on the canvas
To pass into its hourglass
And the artist quick to the heart by symbols
Gifted with trust hesitates:
Is the stone finer in the wall?

BLUE MORAINE in evening's glacier

The vines shade into green, blue takes over the
sky, soil blends in earth, red
builds and absorbs the fields of Crau.
Colours are freed from objects and
recover the dense autonomy that was theirs
before objects, like the clay predating Adam

Saurian earth emerges and lifts its fangs
to the moon, dreamy years steal from their caverns
and tenderly prowl around its thick hide Cliff
rears, Victory resumes his epoch for the night. Even
the clouds part, quitting them.

   This quaking earth hurriedly deserted
they huddle in the town, bucklered by doors.

LE CIEL comme un enfant monte en haut des arbres
l'eau devenue senteur
                              traverse
les fleurs s'appellent Danaé dans le lit

le bruit de Rome dans les cimes
                                    oscillantes
ivres insectes   tonnelle des cris
et le soleil mis en sacs légers ici
et là
la peau s'irrite
beauté d'arbre comme un cheval musclé sur la mare
plus loin l'école de danse des jeunes pommiers

                    RANGEMENT du soir
Le soleil au bout comme un chaudron de cuivre
Autour la plinthe mer qui n'éblouit
Les choux la cloche les alouettes sous
   le rose et le bleu de château là-haut
      Qu'est-ce la paix
Les pommes distinctes en papier peint
Tonneaux de nuages lie roulés en contre-bas
La lampe des dahlias s'allume
L'odeur de cuisson a forme de village
Mais il ne faut que la paix du poème
   soit trop courte

PHASES ÉVÉNEMENTS demi-voltes
Ellipses centaures prolepses cercles voltes
Elisions masques détails fuites instantanés
Comparaisons déplacements hyperboles explosions
Pointes quatre-coins passages câbrements
Colin-maillards figements torsions apostrophes
Equerres saute-moutons voilements ocelles
Véroniques thmèses écarquillements mimétisme
Pointes glissements synecdoques pas-de-deux
Grands-soleils jeters saluts quartes moues
Quart-de-tour supposition premiers-quartiers métonymie
Septimes paris grands-écarts bluffs ombres chinoises
Qui tendent à l'orateur sous son silence la figure

   Vous appelez ça comparaison ?

THE SKY'S a child climbs up the trees
water turning to perfume
                              saunters through
the flowers' name is Danaë in bed

the noise of Rome in the heights
                                    waving
drunken insects   arbour of cries
and the sunshine in packets here
and there
the skin itches
tree's beauty a sinewy horse on a green pond
further off a dancing-school of young appletrees

            CLEARING away evening
Sun at one end like a copper cauldron
The skirting-board sea unglittering
Cabbages, bell and larks under
   the castle-pink and blue up there
      What's peace
A wallpaper of crisp apples
Barrels of dreg-coloured cloud rolled low
The dahlia lamps light up
The smell of cooking's shaped like a village
But the poem's peace must not
   be too short

PHASES HAPPENINGS demivoltes
Ellipses centaurs circles voltes elisions
Prolepses details escapes comparisons
Displacements masks hyperboles explosions
Passages shyings congealments apostrophes
Blindman's buff ocelli landslips leapfrogs
Veronicas tmeses concealments synecdoches
Stares casts greetings parries grimaces
Pig-in-the-middle assumption metonymy
Stills torsions cartwheels points
Quarter-turns mimetism somersaults twosteps
Splits bluffs septimes wagers shadow-plays
Behind the speaker's silence offer their figures

   You call all that comparison ?

JEAN PÉROL
Yorou: la nuit

IL SE traque, il se malmène, il craque. C'est pour le pas de
celui ou de celle qui court sur sa route la nuit. Le pas, le bruit du
pas, font du sur place dans son attente. Il est trop seul, trop
bien. Féroce? Trop couturé dedans par des batailles bêtes.
Aux barbelés imaginaires s'est-il assez coupé! Quand la terre
s'arrondit comme une dune . . . Il s'étend. Un ciel laiteux
d'étoiles lui ponce la poitrine. Torse nu dans le sable, il plaque
son dos au froid d'éther des coquillages morts. Sa vie, sa vie
d'ici, sur de la vie au loin. Au-dessus de lui une femme jeune
ouvre une chevelure noire et des yeux immobiles contre la
nuit mouvante. Elle a replié sous la tête de l'homme ses jambes
accueillantes; le vent de mer fraîchit ses bras étroits. Ils
parlent, franchissant des mensoges en trois langues différentes.
Solitaires à bord de monde, la barre lourde, la barre blanche
des vagues scande leur calme au fond de l'ombre. A la maraude
du bonheur où sont-ils arrivés? 'Off limits you are off limits',
leur dit la voix qui n'est pas Dieu mais officier américain. La
voiture lente braque ses phares blancs sur deux petites ombres
debout, silhouettes épinglées contre une ronde.

Kikou: le chrysanthème

LÀ-BAS LA fleur de mort, ici la fleur de vie. A la roue des mers
les ideés changent. Lui, il revoit dans ce friselis blanc du
chrysanthème un peu du givre de novembre. Là-bas, dès le
matin, le silence baissait les yeux au coin des rues. Des femmes
noires s'acheminaient vers la forêt des croix, en épiant le
bouquet des autres du coin de l'oeil. Des femmes noires, et
chapeautées, et corsetées. La tête comme le coeur, carré. Ici
l'amante au milieu de la nuit arrache un chrysanthème du
bouquet. Elle se tend, nue, au travers du lit—et les pointes
épaisses des seins tremblent un peu—pour atteindre la fleur.
Qu'elle donne à l'homme, au torse de l'amour. Tout à coup
au-dessus de la terre, la mort, l'amour, moussent ensemble dans
ce nid de pétales. Trente secondes, une minute, le sommet
blanc de cette joie. Un pas de pointes, la vie tourne. C'est pour
cela qu'il se laisse durer. Pour qu'apparaisse encore, parfois,
un soir, de ce qui semble noir et glacé, cet envers de neige qui
a le goût des lèvres . . .

Yoru: Night

HE TRACKS himself, maltreats himself, he cracks. For the step of man or woman running night's road. The step, the footfall, make a then and there in his waiting. He's too alone, too at ease. Fierce? Too scarred inside with idiotic battles. So much cut about by imaginary barbed wire. When earth rounds off like a dune . . . He lies down. A star-milky sky sandpapers his body. Bare-chested in the sand, he lies down flat upon the ether-chill of dead shells. His life, his life here, upon far-off life. Above him a young woman opens black hair and un-moving eyes to the moving night. She has tucked her welcoming legs under his head; the sea wind cools her thin arms. They talk, spanning lies in three different languages. Lonely aboard the world, the heavy surf, waves' white surf in rhythm with their deep-shadowed calm. What point have they reached in the plunder of happiness? 'Off limits you are off limits,' says a voice which is not God but an American officer. The slow car levels its white headlights on two small standing shadows, silhouettes pinned against a halo.

Kiku: Chrysanthemum

THERE THE flower of death, here the flower of life. On the wheel of the seas, notions alter. He sees in the chrysan-themum's white quivering a little November frost. There, from morning onwards, silence lowered its eyes at street-corners. Women in black set off to the forest of crosses, looking askance at each other's wreaths. Women in black, in hats, in corsets. Heads like hearts, box-shaped. Here, the beloved at dead of night tears a chrysanthemum from the bouquet. She stretches naked across the bed—the blunt nipples of her breasts tremble a little—to reach the flower. Which she gives to the man, to the shoulders of love. At once above the earth, death and love are rumpled together in this nest of petals. Thirty seconds, a minute, white summit of this joy. A tiptoed step, life turns. For this, he permits himself to last. So that again, sometimes, some evening, out of what seems dark and frozen, there may appear an underside of snow tasting of lips.

Les flagelles d'avril

PLUS VITE, plus vite! Quelquefois le réel rattrape les symboles. Les frêles fleurs de l'éphémère, leurs pétales, leur peau de femme sortant du bain, meurent plus vite sous les délires en rafales. La pluie, ses lanières plaquées, les bourrasques brûleuses jaillies salées de la mer, rongent, arrachent, emportent. Acide est le sillon qui passe entre tes seins, la goutte qui s'y glisse, acide est cette veine sur ton poignet brisé. Frissons violents des cerisiers: trop tendres, trop neuves, toutes leurs fleurs éparpillées. Acide, acide le printemps, ses branches, ses dessins, acide ta minceur, acides les deux bords de tes hanches avides, acide mon regret de ne pas t'embrasser, t'embrasser, nue, vive, ruisselante, dans la glaise, sous les fouets de la pluie, sous la pluie des pétales, jusqu'où s'en vont les cadavres de chair, les cadavres de fleurs . . .

Le vainqueur

DES HEURES qui ne comptent plus ouvrent leurs pétales sur ton poignet. Quelle heure est-il? celle de la pluie pour rien, des pages pour rien et des rues pour rien. Alors celui-là le proclame: 'Christ me montre tout du doigt. A genoux, à genoux! J'avance. Je suis divin comme mes mots et mes visions.' Il prend quelques notes sans écouter, car il a déjà trouvé, son monde est le bon, sa terre sûre, et sa foi la meilleure. Les grossiers, les rebutés, les athées, les jaunes, les noirs, assis, se taisent en le regardant passer. Sa soutane brille: Dieu. Son carnet est blanc: Dieu. Son stylo va vite: Dieu. Avec le dernier mot qu'il a toujours, il disparaît. Il ne reste plus qu'à reprendre son crochet, à fouiller dans les heures qui ne comptent plus.

L'envie

UN RHINOCÉROS crève la muraille. Les bulldozers jaunes et noirs, la pelleteuse à dents de tigre, anéantissent les vieux murs. A gestes amples, des hommes dressés en tuent les pans à coups de masse. Un peu plus loin tournent les grues, des chalumeaux pressés façonnent des étraves, un pétrolier rouge et blanc fend lentement une baie bleue. Les mains s'emploient, la peau ruisselle, l'univers obéit. Sur les couleurs crues des travaux, la poussière monte, et le soleil.   *over*

The April Flagella

FASTER, FASTER! Sometimes reality catches up with symbols. The fragile flowers of transience, their petals, their complexion a woman's stepping from the bath, die sooner under gusts of frenzy. The rain, its thongs slapping down, its scorching flurries bursting salty from the sea, erode, uproot, erase. Acid is the cleft between your breasts, the raindrop running there, acid the vein on your upturned wrist. The cherry-trees' shuddering thrill: too frail, too fresh, all their flowers scattered. Acid, acid the spring, its branches, its patterns, acid your thinness, acid both sides of your greedy hips, acid my regret for not kissing you, kissing you, naked, vivid, drenched, in the loam under the lashes of rain, the rain of petals, to where the corpses of flesh go, the corpses of flowers.

The Conqueror

HOURS THAT no longer count open their petals at your wrist. What's the time? the time of rain for nothing, pages for nothing, streets for nothing. Then *he* proclaims: 'Christ's finger points to me. On your knees, on your knees! I approach. I am divine like my words and my visions.' He jots down a few notes without listening, for he knows already, his world is right, his earth steady, his faith the best. The profane, the reprobates, the atheists, the yellow races and the black, sit silently watching him pass. His cassock has a sheen: God. His note-book is white: God. His pen races: God. With his inevitable last word, he vanishes. There's nothing left to do but pick up one's knitting, and rummage among the hours that no longer count.

Envy

A RHINOCEROS breaches the rampart. Sabre-toothed steam-shovel, black and yellow bulldozers, annihilate the old walls. With vigorous sledgehammer blows, erect men murder the fragments. Further off cranes turn, hasty blow-lamps build stemposts, a red and white tanker slowly cleaves through a blue bay. Hands are busy, skin pours sweat, the universe obeys. Over the raw colours of the building site, dust and sunlight climb.

Mais à l'étage, entre les hommes et la mer, quelle humilité inaperçue peine au labeur dans leurs rumeurs ? Change-t-on les murs de l'âme ? livre-t-on de l'énergie ? Sur du papier blanc, une plume écrit. Sans sueur sans poussière sans salaire et sans bruit, l'inefficace inusable dans l'invisible se construit.

Brasseurs de pierre, fendeurs d'acier, par moment je vous envie.

Salutaire

LES HOMMES dans l'enfance s'enferment à double tour. A travers leurs souvenirs on les entend souffler. Ont-ils peur de s'exposer, ont-ils peur de brûler ? Buter chaque jour au coin des mêmes rues, tirer soir par soir entre la chance et soi le seul ciel qui nous ait déformés, ne leur fait donc pas sourdre aux commissures des lèvres la mousse acide des nausées ? Mustang ou chien, quel espace entre deux sorts, quel désarroi ! Filer, faire gicler l'écume salée, se dépouiller, crépiter, brusquer la vie à chaque pas, lève les craintes si haut et si multiples qu'elles retombent sur eux et les recouvrent. La sagesse devient le clos, la sagesse c'est le couché. Or mourir dans le petit, assez ! Ah les anges gentils, il faut s'arrêter de leur dire oui. Une seule fois dans ta vie, l'ange que tu fus, qu'il vole, mais qu'il vole en éclats. Il faut bombarder les vocables anciens, et ange enfance ou passé, il faut franchir et renier.

La mémoire

POÈMES SUR la mort, sur l'enfance, vous mentez toujours un peu. La lumière est d'argent, d'un gris de cendres illuminées, et toute réflexion faite, un brouillard d'été joyeux. Un paysage n'est pas un homme, la coupure demeure et s'élargit infranchissable entre les deux, les symboles dans la main qui les retourne montrent leur face dérisoire. Cependant je suis brume, je vis brume, j'ai toujours légèrement flotté comme un voile provisoire sur les baies, sur les îles de la vie. La vérité qui se sonde renvoie des ondes vagues en écho : mes souvenirs fondent plus vite que la glace au plein soleil, je me retrouve là, je m'étonne chaque matin d'être là, clos dans un point, puis je me glisse dans un autre qui se referme et coupe tous les ponts, vrai, je n'arrive pas à comprendre le temps, mes heures, mes crans d'arrêt qui

over

But midway, between men and sea, what unperceived humility toils in their noise? Can the walls of the soul be rebuilt? Can you deliver a batch of energy? A pen writes on a blank sheet. With no sweat no dust no payment and no sound, the inadequate imperishable builds in the invisible.

Stone-mixers, steel-cutters, sometimes I envy you.

Salutary

MEN DOUBLE-LOCK themselves in childhood. Through their memories you hear them panting. Are they afraid to expose themselves, afraid of burning? Colliding every day at the same street-corners, evening after evening drawing between chance and themselves the one heaven that has de-formed us, doesn't this force nausea's bitter froth from the corners of their lips? Mustang or dog, what a gulf between two destinies, what disarray! Running off, splashing up salty foam, stripping, crackling, hustling life at every step, raises so many fears so high that they collapse and cover them. Wisdom becomes enclosure, wisdom is lying down. Enough of dying in narrowness! You must stop saying yes to obliging angels. For once in your life, let the angel you were, fly, yes, fly to pieces. Bombard the old words, span and renounce the angel of childhood or past.

Memory

POEMS ON death, on childhood, you always falsify a bit. The light is silver, the grey of light on cinders, and come to think of it, a happy summer's fog. A landscape's not a man, the rift remains and widens impassable between, the symbols in the hand that turns them over show their absurd side. Yet I'm mist, I live mist, I've always tenuously floated like a passing veil over life's bays and islands. Truth sounds itself out, sends back vague echo-waves: my memories melt faster than ice in bright sunlight, I'm here again, amazed every morning I'm here again, sealed within a point, then slide into another which closes and burns all its bridges, true, I can't get a grasp on time, my hours, my safety-catches clicking off. Others, life,

se décalent. Les autres, ma vie, les siècles, l'enfant que peut-
être je fus, l'histoire : je me pince le bras, je mets le doigt sur le
point. Je suis là, tout le reste je rêve, puisque de repère en
repère je m'éveille désarçonné, ouvrant des mains où jamais
je ne tiens rien. O soleil qui s'élève qui s'efface et qui revient,
point fixe autour duquel nous vieillissons . . .

JACQUES ROUBAUD
ennemie

Au vert remué où tendent tes bas rouges
résine des chairs et pavot touffu et sexe
ennemie tu m'emportes   ennemie rieuse
au vert qui siffle   (dos rond   arrosée d'yeuses
odeur de rosée de la seule aube fixe)
tu caches lavandes   sorbes dans ta bouche

ennemie   me ruines   rêvant de me fondre
au creux   boucles   de ton palais abyssant
pareil aux roses d'ausone qui me font
cesser le monde pour/   (seigneur de rencontre
    en épées   jaillissant)

j'ai vu mille morts et le seul mort c'est moi   reins raidis sous
une échelle enneigée   bouche violacée sur le tapis soudain
rongé d'une braise perdant mon corps   perdant la boue et la
chaleur   parfois   vous m'accrochez de votre gaffe dans
l'eau

mort   j'ai trempé dans tous les godets du temps   bu ses
bières sous les tables   troqué de sa jeunesse au bal de la
feuille rouge de l'étamine   dans mes os de cidre je sens
vieillir mes herbes   vieillir en poudre   les pas plus rares sur
ma tête

à quoi bon opposer au monde une morale inchangée   une vie
malléable un courage réticent   et ne lutter jamais que forcé
dans son cœur à quoi bon

j'ai été mort de tout temps   j'en ai porté tous les masques
    grimaçant s'il fallait   tranquille s'il fallait   sinon
comment aurais je su mourir ?

centuries, the child perhaps I was, history: I pinch my arm, I
place my finger on the spot. I'm here, the rest I dream,
since from landmark to landmark I wake my bearings lost,
opening hands that hold nothing. O sun rising, fading, return-
ing, fixed point round which we age . . .

she-enemy

In the confused green where your red stockings offer
resin of flesh and tufted poppy and sex
enemy you take me   laughing enemy
in the whistling green   (back bowed   sprinkled with oak
dew-smell of the one fixed dawn)
concealing lavender   sorbs in your mouth

enemy   destroying me   dreaming of melting me
in the hollow   curls   of your abyssing palace
like the roses of ausonius which make me
cease the world to/ ·   (lord of meeting
    in swords   spurting)

i've seen a thousand deaths and the one death is myself   spine
rigid under a snowed-up ladder   purple mouth on the carpet
suddenly gnawed by embers losing my body   losing the
mire and the warmth   sometimes   you hook me in the
water with your gaffe

dead   i've dipped in all the bowls of time   drunk its beers
under the table   swapped its youth at the dance of the red leaf
of the stamen   in my cider bones i feel   my grasses ageing
    ageing to dust   steps rarer above my head

what's the good of confronting the world with an unchanged
morality   a malleable life a tactful courage   and never
struggle but forced in one's heart what's the good

i've been dead for ever   i've worn all its masks   making
faces if i had to   calm if i had to   otherwise   how would i
have known how to die?

le ciel joint a mouvement   et les ans   ont mouvement   sur
l'échiquier   les   tours   déjà   bougées   ce   que   les   yeux   ne
saisiront qu'avec retard   capables du guet continu des signes
jamais

car la moins diamant des couleurs quand   elle goutte comme
ivresse d'acide sur la craie   c'est le bond des étoiles   perçu
avec fol retard   un coup d'aurore crié qui défoncera le noir

ainsi de l'âge avec   plus là sans recours   sans l'illusion de
matins qui s'aperçoivent sur la spirale ou   deux saisons de
même nom que nous disons se ressembler

l'ombre qui va droit   qui nous engouffre   les yeux encore
chauds du soleil   nous entrons dans la zone du soir vécu
sous nos paupières persistent les vagues colorées

à la fin oublie l'enfance ses oreilles de chien   les jeux de
cinquante   deux   images   qui   se   répètent   toute   expérience
n'est que miette dans la mandibule énorme qui nous happe
pourquoi   marcher à reculons retourne toi il n'y a rien

devant   sinon un pouce d'espace qui se fige à mesure que
nous l'abordons on dit l'avenir et certains voient une plaine
d'autres pas   c'est une question peu soluble à laquelle nous
savons donner de belles réponses funambulesques: premiers
pas dans le presque sûr qui deviendra vite le sûrement ensuite
je ne sais qui ne deviendra pas moins certain

les heures nous avalent l'une après l'autre   on ne s'attardera
pas dans les parages on attendra que l'écorce se grave d'elle-
même sur le canif   qui saurait patienter autrement   les
lendemains s'accrochent comme limailles

chacun est emporté parallèlement   tu regardes   tu regardes
tant que tu mourras de rire   trottoirs   allumettes   pioches
    savons   planches   monnaies   se   voilent   s'oblitèrent
s'effilochent   s'embuent   se délitent

le mieux serait de changer de lumière   de vivre dans l'œil de
deux grains de sable qui s'écartent   d'être un seul banc vert
                                                                    over

the joined sky has movement   and the years   have move-
ment   castles already moved on the chessboard   which the
eyes grasp only with a time-lag   capable of always watching
the never signs

for the least diamond of colours when   it drips like acid
intoxication on the chalk   is the leap of stars   perceived
with crazy time-lag   a shouted burst of aurora staving in the
blackness

it's the same with age   no   more   there irremediably
without the illusion of mornings perceiving each other on the
spiral or   two namesake seasons that we say are alike

the shadow moving straight ahead   engulfing us   eyes still
warm with sunlight   we enter the zone of evening lived
through   behind our eyelids persist the coloured waves

well forget childhood its dog-ears   the play of fifty-two
images repeating themselves   any experience is just a crumb
in the huge mandible that snaps us up why   walk backwards
turn round there's nothing

in front   if not an inch of space freezing as we enter it we say
the future and some see a plain   others not   it's a question
hard to solve and we give it fine tightropewalking answers:
first steps in the almost certain which will rapidly become the
certainly then i don't know which will not become less certain

the hours swallow us one after another   we won't have to
wait in the whereabouts we'll wait for the bark to carve itself
on the penknife   which would know how to wait anyway
tomorrows hook onto each other like iron filings

everyone's carried off in parallel   you look   you look until
you die of laughing   pavements   matches   picks   soap
boards   small change   are   dimmed   obliterated   un-
ravelled   steamed over   dissolved

it would be best to change lights   to live in the eye of two
grains of sand parting   to be a single green layer in more or
over

dans plutôt le désert printemps central   à toujours cinq
heures du matin

le mieux   si du moins il peut exister un mieux pour l'appro-
fondissement du désert toujours le même   (autruche
rapetissée jusquà être l'œuf du pigeon   ou goutte d'eau
étirée jusqu'à l'infinitude du rail)

le mieux serait alors résolument immobile   fixer la pierre
quand elle trempe l'acier de l'eau   (une bouche va s'ouvrir
et vibrer jusqu'au désordre)

si l'on pouvait aliéné absolu   durer   prendre pied en un
point comme Loth pétrifié dans trois mémoires de sel blanc

ce n'est pas vrai   je mens   tout est faux   il n'y a rien en
arrière   je ne suis pas du monde   je ne suis pas non plus du
monde que j'étais   je ne vis pas   un mort me glace le
vécu   j'avance sous absence   je suis le

chapitre zéro du livre   la basse oubliée dans la partition
économisant le vide   enchaînant des raisons qui n'assurent
rien   je ne suis même pas retranché je suis nul   dépossédé
du don d'échange

on a conclu pour moi dans le même temps où je posais mon
premier axiome blanc contre noir   et la phrase roule où rien
ne signifie

quelque part je ne vois plus   ou autrement peut-être autre-
ment qui rendra le vrai vrai   le noir noir   ouvrira les yeux
sur autre que la mort ?

petit tamis pour pépites petit   petit remous dans la grande
eau blanche   petit   menu foin menus celliers   fontaine
devant les chutes   petit cahier où se lira petit morceau de
craie petite fable   petit marbre sous petit if taillé bas   petite
histoire pauvrement

malheur pas malin   bouche cousue   pauvreté confusion
pierres   petite morale d'agneau bâté   petits habitants de
polenta de panurgie petits ports d'anchois et d'ail   petite
porte des lionnes à Mycènes

over

less the desert central spring   at permanently five o'clock in
the morning

best   that is if there can be a best for the better understanding
of the always same desert   (ostrich diminished to pigeon's
egg   or waterdrop drawn out to a rail's infinity)

it would be best then resolutely motionless   to fix the stone
when it steeps steel with water   (a mouth will open and
vibrate to the point of disorder)

if one could estranged absolute   last   take one's stand on a
point like Lot petrified in three memories of white salt

it's not true   i'm lying   it's all false   there's nothing
behind it   i don't belong to the world   i don't belong to the
world that i did either   i'm not living   a dead freezes my
lived   i move in absence   i am the

chapter nought of the book   the bass left out of the score
saving up the non-existent   building a chain of thought that
assures of nothing   i'm not even subtracted i'm nothing
dispossessed of the gift of exchange

it was settled for me at that moment when i set my first axiom
white against black   and the sentence travels on to where
nothing means

somewhere i can't see any more   or else perhaps else who
will make the real real   the black black   open the eyes on
what is not death?

little sieve for nuggets little   little eddy in the big white
water   little   small hay small pantries   spring before the
falls   little notebook where you read little scribble of chalk
little fable   little marble under little yew cut back   little
story poorly

silly   mishap   not a word   poverty confusion stones
little horizons of perfect crass   little dwellers in pasta in
sheepland little ports of anchovies and garlic   little lioness
portal in Mycenae

pentes de l'or et pentes du vin   petits sous tassés petitement
    légère mousse d'un autrement   d'un ailleurs   petit
argent de la jeunesse petit plomb de la fatigue

presque pas   peu à peu   à peine   par hasard   parcelle
hôpital corridor   mots petits   presque-mots   paille
plainte peureux   petits désastres   petits   petit monde

JACQUES GARELLI
Annexion

T O U T P O È M E doit annexer un paysage, réseau tendu de la course inaudible des sphères, au cycle périodique des saisons. Né de la gorge, par son rythme lacuneux, le poème fonde.

C'est le champ de fusion des couleurs jusqu'alors injurieuses, des matières qui se désagrègent, des liaisons incompatibles parce que méchantes et sonores.

Lieu de rencontre entre la volonté farouche de l'animal et l'inertie de craie, en lui, la terre jusqu'alors muette, vire et change.

C'est la zone dynamique qui gronde vers un terme toujours futur. C'est le monde aveugle du squale qui bourdonne dans l'assourdissement du plongeon.

JUDE STÉFAN
La cabane du berger

A B A N D O N N É E S U R la lande déserte
aux nuées et aux regards du Temps
la roulotte de berger fait penser
le Voyageur au Poète fervent
qui jadis inventa sa beauté
son destin; inhabitée vide
de toutes les piétés de la femme
elle repose incomprise au sol
penchée les roues empêtrées
là stoïque sur la terre de prose.

Jude et Judith

—E T L ' H I V E R Jude ?—L'hiver est oubli
du printemps là encore sous la neige   *over*

slopes of gold and slopes of wine   little pennies piled small
slight pother of an otherwise   otherwhere   little credit of
youth little debit of tiredness

Almost not   bit by bit   barely   by chance   allotment
hospital corridor   little words   almost-words   straw
moan frightened   little accidents   little   little world

Annexation

EVERY POEM must annex a landscape, taut network of the
unheard movement of the spheres, to the periodic cycle of
the seasons. Born in the throat, by its intermittent rhythm,
the poem founds.

It is the field of fusion of colours till then outrageous, of
materials in disintegration, of conjunctions that are incompat-
ible since wicked and sonorous.

Meeting-place of the animal's fierce will and chalk's inertia,
through it the previously dumb world veers and alters.

It is the dynamic zone growling towards an always future
term. It is the shark's blind world buzzing in the deafness of
the plunge.

The Shepherd's Hut

ABANDONED ON the empty moor
to clouds and the gaze of Time
the shepherd's caravan reminds
the Traveller of the fervent Poet
who once invented its beauty
its destiny; uninhabited empty
of a woman's pieties
it rests uncomprehended on the ground
canted its wheels hobbled
stoical there on the prose earth.

Jude and Judith

—AND WINTER Jude ?—Winter forgets
spring still there under snow

des lilas (O temps blanc lugubre
ministère comme un baiser ressemble
à la haine violenté sur belles lè-
vres abjectes de maraude écrasée
contre un arbre tandis que rauques
en lent cri volettent les corneilles
elle l'œil et la chair moi leur bat-
tante hantise !)—Et ces justes noms
d'été d'automne ?—La passion de mûrir
puis de flétrir déjà.

L'or de leur corps

COMME EN ton coffre la servante cherche
à toute pose plus riche parure
—et moi témoin sûr en la glace—
ainsi m'invite ta blancheur à mal-
adroitement ému puis avec habitude
la fouiller et tes lèvres les mouiller
plus suave et plus vite cherchant
des mains aveugles et baisers en son
réduit ce trésor jamais extrait
mais alors derechef convoitable
sang doux tes seins à ma fatigue.

Étreinte

MA PURE et violentée pardonne
qu'il me faille encore par souci
de mort en ce terrible été cru
épuiser l'eau de tes lèvres cher-
cher au profond de ton aine le frais
à la brûlure je ne te veux pas
humiliée mais toi pourquoi me ser-
rer à mort gisante grâciante
mais pourquoi mourir de nous aimer
en baisers en cris en ces larmes
blanches du corps qui l'assouvissent
après le fardeau de tant de marches ?
Je ne sais je n'ai vu que l'émoi
de tes yeux ton insupportable peau.

of lilacs (O white weather dismal
ministry as a kiss resembles
hate plundered from love-
ly abject lips of a slut you crush
against a tree while raucous
slow-cawing circle the rooks
she eye and flesh I their obsess-
ive pulse!)—And those right names
of summer and autumn?—Passion to ripen
then to as quickly wither.

The Gold of their Bodies

AS THE maid ransacks your coffer for
a richer dress for every pose
—and I a faithful witness in the mirror—
so your whiteness invites me to
clumsily moved and then conversantly
explore it moistening your lips
smoother and quicker seeking with
blind hands and kisses in its
redoubt the treasure never mined
but then forthwith desirable
sweet blood your breasts to my exhaustion.

Embrace

MY PURE and violated love forgive
that I should once again by fret
of death this raw and raging summer
suck dry the water of your lips and seek
deep in your groin to slake
this burning I do not desire you
humiliated but you why clutch
me to death stretched out grace-granting
why should we die of loving one another
in kisses cries and in these white
tears of the body sating the body
after such heavy load of stairs?
I cannot tell I've only seen your eyes'
emotion unendurable your skin.

Tombeau

VOUS QUI survivez les encore de-
bout sur nos cadavres ne venez pleu-
rer ni patelinement vous recueil-
lir trop tard où ne germe pas même
un grain d'éternité n'ayant nous-mêmes
été qu'une fois au sol tombés dé-
livrés des vivants pullulants et de
toutes sublimes sornettes. Pour
mémoire une croix pour vérité
le vide entre boue et nuées béant
pour amour des abois perdus à la lune
des hiboux narguant l'éternelle aube
des jours. Ci-gît qui fut court temps
debout avec son rire.

Belle veuve

AU LIEU de l'énfouir au froid du sol si
tu conservais mon corps dans la saumure
où ? mais dans un tonneau dans la cave
alors plus éternellement certes tu
tirerais les courtines de notre
chaude commune couche notre vie
durant—or l'ennui sur les murs n'en suin-
terait-il pas moins qui jaunit nos faces
odieuses trop vite mûries si bien
que mieux vaut à ton gré m'accompagner
ou me survivre longuement marchant
par les bois du regret oui le plus long-
temps possible piétinant le malheur
de ma rencontre.

Tomb

YOU WHO survive still stand-
ing upon our corpses do not come
to weep or mealy-mouthed repent
too late where seeds not even
one grain of eternity for we've
existed only once fallen to earth de-
livered from the close-packed living
and all solemn rigmarole. For
memory a cross for truth
the space between mud and clouds agape
for love lost baying at the moon
of owls taunting the days' etern-
al dawn. Here lies who was brief time
erect and with its laughter.

Beautiful Widow

INSTEAD OF interring in earth's cold if
you preserved my body in brine
where ? but in a barrel in the cellar
for sure then more eternally you
could draw the curtains of our
warm common bed while our lives
last—then on the walls would boredom
not sweat less yellowing our hateful
faces ripened too quick so that
it's better as you like to go with me
or else to long outlive me walking
through woods of sorrow yes as long
as possible trampling the ill-luck
of meeting me.

DENIS ROCHE

Au début des petits bruits de percussion s'élevaient
Dans un mouvement d'aller et de venue intéressant
Mis—les bruits sont souvent des constats—
—orge froissée ne trouve plus sa justification ne
Devrait plus lui suffire alors qu'à pleines mains
Il tire les hauts des bas de nylon la soupesant
Ainsi masse charmante qui plonge à la verticale dans
L'étoffe, consciencieuse comme est après tout son
Désir. La percussion c'est le spectacle et, une
Fois le théâtre enlevé, il va lui rester ce front
Incliné sur un certain nombre de pensées dirigées
Vers eux seuls (donc elle et moi), dirigées vers
Leur image accouplée que décidément le silence éf-
Face/

                    après déjeuner, deux années après, alors qu'il avaiT
                            appris à l'arrière au front en selle à dé-
                        plier la bâche, à rêver: 'est-il celui qu'iL
                          aurait voulu être un jour? Nulle parT
             et pendant un bon moment après un déjeuner pareiL
                   ne sont-elles pas déjà assises à nos places, leS
                     réservoirs silos poudriers emballeuses assises,
                     les regardent, les remplissent et les conduisE
                 nt à la chapelle rurale. Si possible je les ferA
                 i descendre à la plage, juste devant l'entrée dE
               Qui fait tressaillir l'esprit d'indicibles onduL
           ations? Ah . . . ——————————QuI
                     Ah . . . L'amante s'écroulanT
             SeS bras nus roulent comme une torche qui sE
         transformerait brusquement en une machine partiellE
         d'oscillateur cathodique = un pied d'lampe spiralé O
               Si elle ne se contentait pas de se découraG
             d'se découvrir les seins à chaque occasion dE
       m'embrasser quand je l'éveille en plein somme quand j'ar
       ticule avec soin un arrangement de jambes une posturE
                         après ses excuses
             quelle pourrait être ma mine sinon de filoN
       jaunissant, d'ordure ou d'héritage en carrosse mal calé
                                                            ?

TO BEGIN with little percussive sounds arose
In an interesting to-and-fro movement
Put—noises are often affidavits—
—ière's crumpling no longer seems justified should no
Longer satisfy him as with both hands
He pulls on the tops of her nylon stockings thus
Weighing the charming mass of her plunging vertically into
The material, conscientious as after all his
Lust is. The percussion is the show and, on-
Ce the theatre's removed, there will remain this forehead
Bent over a certain number of thoughts directed
On them alone (i.e. her and me), directed towards
Their coupled image that silence decidedly ef-
Faces/

After lunch, two years later, when he haD
learnt at the rear at the front in the saddle to un-
fold the tarpaulin, to dream: "is he the one hE
would have wished one day to be? NowherE
and for some time after such a luncH
aren't they already sitting on our seats, thE
reservoirs, silos, powder-compacts, stunners sitting,
look at them, fill them and take theM
to the country chapel. If possible I shA

il take them down to the beach, just in front of the way in tO
Who makes the spirit tremble with indescribable unduL
ations? Ah . . . ——————————— WhO

Ah . . . My mistress flops dowN
and HeR bare arms thresh like a torch thaT
changes suddenly into the partial mechanisM
of a cathode oscillator $=$ a spiralled lamp-standard O
If she weren't happy to get tirE
of uncovering her breasts on every occasioN

kissing me when I waken her during her forty winks when I ca
refully articulate an arrangement of legs a posturE
after her excuses
I couldn't look like anything but a piece of cakE
going yellow, ordure or inheritance like a badly-chocked carriage
?

Il n'a pourtant pas le genre à atte
Hors à la regarder, à—que le lec
La reconnaître, à qui vient d'êt
Passants dans le camp opposé, v
Cousu dans ton fil blanc d'am
'Allons donc, cela n'est qu'
Très bon d'en reparler, milli
De vêtements distribués … on
Mal 'arriver le plus en aval
Distance au plus loin possib
Moment de repartir nous soyon
Tin! A porter une culotte sur
Somptueuse hôtesse qui regarde, i
Colon, fermier ou le maître de céans ri
Ane ayant beaucoup ri. (Lexique, page 192 et sq comme

CACHÉS

                                                    Pleynet
'Hôtesse demeurant accoudée au niveau où elle peut voir
                                                    qu'on ne l'y
Reprendrait plus en position de lectrice de poème couchée

JEAN-PHILIPPE SALABREUIL
Léproserie d'étoiles

Le soir après la pluie dans mon jardin
Beaucoup de gens battent des mains
Venez monsieur le poète venez voir
Les étoiles sont blanches dans le ruisseau noir
Beaucoup de gens sur l'angle bleu des myosotis
Ont piétiné la bourrée de l'impatience
Et bleui sans vouloir leurs brodequins de cuir
Avec le bleu ma délivrance avec mes myosotis
Venez quand même on a vu pire
On vous demandera pardon avec plein de pervenches
Je me suis donc vêtu de ma très pauvre peau
C'est tout ce que je mets entre le monde et moi
Mon cœur c'est ce qui bat le reste c'est le froid
Inerte était le froid dans le ruisseau
J'y suis allé portant mon cœur qui bouge à peine
Avec eux j'ai marché le long des bœufs chargés de chaînes
Et là-bas le spectacle n'était pas beau vraiment
Les étoiles étaient mortes une main sur la gorge   *over*

YES BUT he's not the sort who'd wait
Except to look at her, to—let the
Recognize her, to one who has ju
Passing into the enemy camp,
Sewn into your white thread
'Come now, that's nothing
Very good talking abou
Of clothes distributed
Badly 'get as far upstre
Distance as far as possible
Moment to leave again let's
Ning! Wearing a pair of pants on
Sumptuous hostess looking, here
Colonialist, farmer or master of the ho
Ass having laughed a lot. (Lexicon, p. 92ff. like
                                                    Pleynet
'Hostess remaining leaning at the level she can see
                                            that she can't be
Taken again in the position of a supine poem-reader

HIDDEN

Leprosy of Stars

AT EVENING in my garden after rain
Lots of people clap their hands
Come mister poet come and see
The stars are white in the black brook
Lots of people on the blue forgetmenot bed
Have been dancing the bourrée of impatience
Not meaning to stain their leather boots blue
With blue my deliverance with my forgetmenots
Come along anyway it's not a bad sight
We'll beg your pardon with lots of periwinkles
So I got dressed up in my poorman's skin
It's all I put between me and the world
My heart is what beats the rest is cold
Inert was the cold in the brook
I went out carrying my barely moving heart
With them I walked beside oxen loaded with chains
And the spectacle wasn't really pretty
The stars were dead with a hand on their throats

Comme font les grenouilles au ventre blanc
Sur la rouille des mares où pisse le bouc jaune
Alors on s'en retourne et seul je suis resté
Je me demande ainsi pourquoi mon cœur remue
Dans les plis de ma peau comme une bête nue
Mais les cornes de bœufs quand je suis repassé
Avaient crevé la nuit que la mort les bénisse
Dans l'angle du jardin l'ombre penchée me glisse
Un pot de lait fleuri avec un bouquet bleu
Il y a aussi dessus un petit hochequeue
Qui tremble et dans ma poche je l'ai mis
Je respire les fleurs et puis je bois le lait
Etoiles après la pluie on sait que je vous aime
Ils me diront demain si je les remercie
C'est rien c'est rien du tout c'est pour ce beau poème
Où vous chantez si bien notre léproserie.

Un petit couloir

UN PETIT couloir de craie blanche
Sur le bord de l'eau bleue qui tremble
Et voici que je marche sans lanterne
Au-devant d'une table dans les étoiles

L'ombre épineuse y tremble et tourne
D'un grand rosier dans la lune lointaine
Et comme dans l'amour de l'âme et des fontaines
Rien ne s'explique plus qu'à grands signes d'eau pâle
Emportés par la nuit vers le mur bleu du fleuve

Amour il fallut que je découvre
Autre usage d'un ongle en ta tempe de craie
Ame profonde sur la blanche baie
Des prairies brumeuses tes yeux de source
Vers elle se tournèrent qu'il faut que je retrouve

Et moi sur la chaise des pervenches nocturnes
Je suis assis mains plates sur la table des herbes
L'eau passe bleue sous la barque qui s'use
Au loin roulent blancs les mondes jusqu'à se perdre.

Like white-bellied frogs
On the rust of ponds where the yellow stag pisses
So they all went away and I'm left there alone
And I wonder why my heart moves
In the pleats of my skin like a naked animal
But on my return the oxen's horns
Had ripped the night open death bless them
At the corner of the garden a crouchback shadow slips me
A jug of milk flowered with a blue bouquet
And on it a little wagtail
That flutters and I put it in my pocket
And smell the flowers and drink the milk
Stars after rain I'm known to love you
If I thank them tomorrow they'll tell me
It's nothing nothing at all it's for this beautiful poem
Where you sing so well of our leprosy.

A Little Corridor

A LITTLE white chalk corridor
Beside the shimmering blue water
And here I am walking with no lantern
Towards a table in the stars

Where trembles and turns the thorny shadow
Of a big rosebush in the far-off moon
And as with love of the soul and of fountains
Nothing can be explained except in vague gestures of pale water
Carried off by night towards the river's blue wall

Love I should have discovered
Other usage for a fingernail in your chalk temple
Deep spirit over the white bay
Of the misty meadows your spring eyes
Turned towards the woman I must find again

And I sit on the chair of the night's blue flowers
My hands are flat on the table of grasses
Blue beneath the ageing boat the water passes
And far-off worlds roll white towards extinction.

Oiseau rouge

TOUT PRÈS le rideau vert
Des pommes et des pommes
Qui tombe sans cesser
Derrière vont les chiens
Chaque chien suit son frère
Ils vont à l'ossuaire
Des lunes apaisées
Je retiens loin du ciel
Mon sang de fin soleil
Oiseau rouge des eaux
Tu dors tu reconnais
La nuit sans ébranler
Au profond de mes sources
Une oreille debout
Amour dans la chênaie
Amour par mille feuilles
A mots obscurs porté
Sur ma paume amollie
Descellant sous la terre
La chaîne lumineuse
A retenir l'été
Sous mon sang la fraîcheur
A libérer les pierres.

Dans la haute année blanche

DANS LA haute année blanche des couronnes
Jetées en craie au ciel de cendres comme
Une tour serait tremblante immaculée de chaux
Par le couloir brisé des branches comme une lampe
Au fond doucement ronde et le lac est plus beau
Plus clair où elle tombe ô fine tempe
A mon épaule je t'aimais fragile ainsi
Radieuse ainsi et menacée mais toute aussi
Dans l'instant secourue plus belle ici vivante
Guérie sans le secours de vie ni de beauté
Mais secours de mort et force obscure lente
(Un désert d'ombre montait au mont du jour d'été)
Je venais je trouvais chemin d'or et de poudre
Au-dessous du passé tourmenté sans résoudre

over

Red Bird

BESIDE ME the green curtain
Of apples and apples
Endlessly falling
Behind it run dogs
Each follows its brother
They're going to the boneyard
Of tranquillized moons
Far from the sky I keep
My pure sun's blood
Red bird of the water
You sleep you recognize
Night without disturbing
Deep at my springs
An ear pricked
Love in the oakwood
Love by a thousand leaves
Carried in enigmatic words
On my softened palm
Unsealing underground
The luminous chain
To imprison summer
Under my blood freshness
To free the stones.

In the High White Year

IN THE high white year of crowns
Cast in chalk into cinder sky like
A tremulous tower immaculately whitewashed
Through the broken corridor of branches like a lamp
Gently rounded below and the lake is more beautiful
Brighter where she falls O delicate temple
On my shoulder I loved you fragile like this
Radiant like this and threatened but also entire
On the instant saved more beautiful here alive
Cured without help of life or beauty
But succour of death and slow dark strength
(A desert of shadow climbed the summer day's hill)
I came I found a path of dust and gold
Under the tormented past without resolving

Le temps ni l'étendue perdus j'ornais venant
De larmes closes l'avenue dès lors fleurie
Je revins il n'est rien de sauvé revenant
Je m'égare à des bords de chute et de furie
Ce n'est que peu qui se maintienne où tout est condamné
Je m'enfonce vois et me perds un gouffre m'est donné
Le soleil en ombrages brûle des bois dans l'âme
Un seul mot désertique épuise le champ du jour
Et l'onde est montée boire aux barques couronnées de flammes
(O combat disais-tu sans fin de l'eau contre le feu)
Je ne t'ai pas trouvée tombé au même amour
Où tu dors allongée dérivante en quels cieux
Je ne peux plus finir un rien me recommence
Une nuit te prenait la mort la terre un monde éteint
Je t'ai cherchée du côté clair de l'avenir immense
Tu portais signe d'aube à la tempe je me souviens.

JEAN PAUL GUIBBERT
Pour Béa

IX

TU AVAIS ô unique martyre en ce jardin,
Les yeux martyrisés, creusés comme l'aisselle,
Et la soie de ton sein gravée de veines crues
Sous le linge de peau aux boucles solennelles.

C'était l'avènement d'un soir bleu et lucide
Et le tain de la glace lançait sur nos éveils
Ses reflets vieillissants de feu de bois;

Ombre mousseuse ce creux d'ombre que je mordais comme
    un fruit vert
Avec les dents de l'impatience,
La peur et le désir de te voir me souffrir.

XVI

J'ai tant aimé tes lèvres que je suis démuni
Et s'il m'arrive par dessein malheureux,
De poser ma bouche sur la pierre,
Il me semble ne plus trouver mes propres lèvres
Et je fuis pour ne point leur rendre le baiser.

Lost time or space in coming I bejeweled
With shuttered tears the avenue then flowered
I returned returning saves nothing
I wander on brinks of falling and frenzy
Only a little can survive where all is sentenced
I sink see and vanish a gulf is given me
The sun in shade burns woods in my soul
A single desert word exhausts the field of day
And a wave has risen to drink the flame-crowned boats
(O endless combat you said of water with fire)
I have not found you I'm trapped by the same love
Where prostrate you sleep drifting in what skies
I cannot end any more a nothing renews me
One night you were taken by death by earth an extinguished world
I've looked for you on the bright side of the vast future
You bore the mark of dawn on your temple I remember.

For Bea

IX

YOU HAD O single martyr in that garden,
Martyred eyes, hollow like the armpit,
And the silk of your breast engraved with rough veins
Under the solemn-curled cloth of skin.

It was the advent of blue and lucid evening
And the mirror's silvering cast on our wakings
Its ageing woodfire reflections;

Mossy shadow that hollow of shadow into which I bit like a
   green fruit
With the teeth of impatience,
The fear and desire of seeing you suffer me.

XVI

I have so much loved your lips that I am recourseless
And if by mischance it should happen
That my mouth touches stone,
I seem no longer to find my own lips
And I escape so as not to return the kiss.

Voix ailée et vaine de Béatrice

I

JE L'AIMAIS, les jours n'étaient que des escales sur des
    îles de fond de mer
Et la lumière de la nuit était celle du fond des eaux
Et nos corps étaient des vaisseaux;

Le lent et perpétuel voyage de nos mains, nos découvertes.

II

Franchi le lieu des eaux et des racines,
Perdue la tige et les corolles consacrées
Je perdais pied;
Lorsque au lointain, à la lisière du lointain,
Dans les lentes contrées
M'apparurent les grands arbres.

Alors me vint l'odeur des feuilles et du sang
Et les gestes de l'Obstiné.

III

Et tu viendras dans ces allées où mon cœur saigne à
    chaque pas
Mes bras seront d'une autre nuit, d'un autre ciel
Et nos embrasements parmi les arbres morts seront d'un
    autre temps;

Et nos arbres et nos bras déchirés vers le ciel
Et les ronces d'enfance et les baies dans nos mains.

IV

Car dans la nuit de notre peur,
Tu aimes avec des larmes dans ta voix
Et la douleur qui est la tienne est sans raison
Et le jeu adorable de l'amour que tu donnes est sans raison
Et toujours je me laisse réduire par ta voix,
Toujours au même ventre je suis grande prêtresse et servante
    de roi
Et la blessure que tu fais à la violence des saisons
Mais le temps après la blessure est une lente floraison,
Une descente au monde bas.

Winged and Futile Voice of Beatrice

I

I LOVED him, the days were but ports of call at
    deepsea islands
And the light of night-time was that of the depths of the
    waters
And our bodies were boats;

The slow perpetual voyage of our hands, our discoveries.

II

Entered the place of waters and roots,
Lost the stem and the sacred corollas
I lost my footing;
When far off, on the verge of distance,
In the languid countries
The tall trees appeared to me.

Then there came to me a scent of leaves and blood
And the gestures of the Obstinate.

III

And you will come to those avenues where my heart at
    every step bleeds
My arms will belong to another night, another sky
And our burning among the dead trees will belong to
    another time;

And our trees and our gashed arms towards the sky
And the brambles of childhood and berries in our hands.

IV

For in the night of our fear,
You love with tears in your voice
And the grief that is yours is without reason
And the adorable play of love that you offer is without
    reason
And always I submit to your voice,
Always to the same bosom I am high priestess and king's
    handmaid
And the wound you make in the violence of the seasons
But after the wound, time is a slow blossoming,
A descent to the world beneath.

Ordre

LES ENFANTS clairs que nous étions
En la saison la plus sereine de l'année
Toute la lumière venant des seins de la bien-aimée;

Un long temps elle m'avait voilé son visage
Soudain ensuite à mon désir
(On ne sait alors quelle ultime misère de nous-même a pu
     fléchir ta résistance, ô merveille).

Cet amour n'est plus,
Et n'est que faim des profondeurs et de taire et de chasser;
L'élan vers elle est sans douceur.
Voici qu'en élan nouveau je marche, et vers les gîtes de la
     peur
Et que ma marche intime est celle de délire.

Cette vie solitaire ne nous est point donnée,
Seul le loisir de déchirer nos solitudes,
D'être nos ombres sans défaut.

Double registre de ce lieu
Dans la lumière de ces arbres;

Ainsi nous avions prévu le triste en ces contrées.
Durant le jour nulle parole de douleur,
Toute misère conjurée,
Nos cœurs pouvaient descendre au repos
(Mais la mort imprévue toujours saborde son élite).

Un silence profond, tout le jour, a habité notre demeure.

JAMAIS FUGUE des eaux,
Hors toujours dans le brisement,
Vers le ténébreux des deltas.

Descendre, toujours (verticale rose)
Et mourir à jamais brisé,
Lassé, bercé, dans l'âme rose.

Jambes nuptiales entravées.

Order

THE CLEAR children we were
In the year's calmest season
The beloved's breasts our sole source of light;

A long time she had veiled her face from me
Sudden then to my desire
(Not knowing what last misery of self could have
    sapped your resistance, O miracle).

This love is no more,
Is only hunger for depths, for concealing and hunting;
The impulse towards her has no gentleness.
And now in a new impulse I walk, and towards the warrens
    of fear
And my inward walking is delirious.

We are not permitted this life alone,
But leave to shatter our solitudes,
To be our own faultless shadows.

Double register of this place
In the light of the trees;

Thus we had foreseen sadness in these lands.
By day no word of sorrow,
All grief conjúred,
Our hearts could sink to rest
(But unforeseen death always sabotages its élite).

Daylong our house has been inhabited by profound silence.

NEVER ESCAPE of waters,
Save always in breaking,
Towards the darkness of deltas.

Descending, always (rose perpendicular)
And dying for ever broken,
Wearied, cradled, in the rose soul.

Nuptial legs fettered.

JADE.

Une blancheur sur les brisants
(anis)
Le tracé mortel du sourcil,
Une branche dans la pupille,
Veines vertes à vos poignets
(bras balancés).

Gestes, sentence inobservée
(la forme sucée de vos lèvres).
La douleur serait si fragile.
Et que sont-elles ?

LE RIRE aussi c'était (ainsi sera)
La fente intense dans le verbe;
Dans le son minéral, le haut vide des voix
Comme prolonge ta parole le silence posé

Quel devenir du jeu d'approche ?
Hormis le bruit d'aimer (j'observe)

Un silence, deux mille années.

JADE.

A whiteness on the breakers
(aniseed)
The mortal line of the eyebrow,
A branch in the pupil,
Green veins at your wrists
(arms poised).

Gestures, sentence suspended
(the sucked shape of your lips).
Pain would be so fragile.
And what are they?

LAUGHTER TOO was (so will be)
The intense fissure in the word;
In mineral sound, voices' high emptiness
As sedate silence prolongs your speech

What progress in the game of closeness?
Except the noise of loving (I observe)

A silence, two thousand years.

Biographies

YVES BONNEFOY (1923–)

Yves Bonnefoy was born at Tours, studied philosophy at the University of Paris, and has, besides his poetry and his essays in criticism, published several exceedingly fine translations of Shakespeare plays. Not surprisingly, he has plenty to say on the differences between French and English poetry. He complains that modern English criticism seeks meaning and sense in poetry, whereas he is more interested in what he calls 'presence'. Consequently it is the essence of the salamander, a life force that the poet identifies with, that is supposed to be present in the poem, rather than its reality as a living reptile.

Bonnefoy's is a poetry of great austerity, his vocabulary and imagery are limited, his tone of uniform splendour. The temptation of 'beauty' is one that he feels very personally: hence his attack on it in poems like 'La beauté'. But see the Introduction for Bonnefoy's *ars poetica*. His fundamental message might be defined as 'In the midst of life we are in death', and his work has immense strength and concentration.

Principal collections of poetry: *Du mouvement et de l'immobilité de Douve*, 1954; *Hier régnant désert*, 1958; *Pierre écrite*, 1965. Essays on poetry: *L'improbable*, 1959; *Un rêve fait à Mantoue*, 1967 (all published by Mercure de France).

ALAIN BOSQUET (1919–)

Born Anatole Bisk, at Odessa. His father, Alexander Bisk, condemned to death during the civil war in the Ukraine, 'owed his freedom to the publication of a collection of poems: for his Tcheka gaoler was a poet'. The family fled to Bulgaria, then Belgium (1925). Alain Bosquet studied Romance philosophy at Brussels Free University, fought with the Belgian and French Armies in the early days of the War, and after the fall of

France went to New York, where he worked on the staff of the Gaullist paper *La Voix de France*. Here he became a friend of André Breton, and collaborated in the Surrealist reviews *VVV* and *View*. In the autumn of 1942 he joined the American Army, and later took part in SHAEF's preparations in London for the Second Front. He worked for the Allies in Germany until 1951, and since then has lived mainly from his writing. He has written 'thousands of newspaper articles', novels as well as poetry, and has translated Brecht, Merrill Moore, Carl Sandburg, Conrad Aiken, Vasko Popa and Lawrence Durrell into French.

For Bosquet, the practice of poetry is an exercise in self-discovery: before writing his poem, the poet's Ego was merely a 'pre-Ego'. Not surprisingly, the *100 notes pour une solitude* (in my view, Bosquet's best collection) are poetry about the writing of poetry. These brief meditations upon creation— written in a never-failing succession of crisp images—deserve to become a set text for aspiring poets !

Principal collections: *La vie est clandestine*, Corrêa, 1945; *A la mémoire de ma planète*, Sagittaire, 1948; *Langue morte* (including *L'image impardonnable* and *Syncopes*), Sagittaire, 1951; *Maître objet*, Gallimard, 1962; *Quatre testaments et autres poèmes* (including *Quel royaume oublié?*), Gallimard, 1967; *100 notes pour une solitude*, Gallimard, 1970.

JEAN BRETON (1930–)

Jean Breton is also a critic of poetry, and is associated with the Librairie Saint-Germain-des-Prés in Paris, whose services to poetry have been and remain considerable. He collaborated with Serge Brindeau in *Poésie pour vivre* (La Table Ronde, 1964), a manifesto for a more popular and less obscure approach to poetry: 'Qu'on perde donc l'habitude de flatter par principe les illisibles et les invisibles, les poètes qui prétendent n'écrire que pour leurs tiroirs et ceux qui ne consentent à être lus, à la rigueur, que par une élite, et sur papier japon. Hommes ordinaires, n'ayant aucune raison de fermer la porte à nos semblables, nous n'estimons pas que l'idéal du poète soit de décourager la lecture ou d'interdire l'approche.' [For goodness' sake let's abandon the habit of flattering, from principle, the unreadable and the invisible, those poets who claim only to write for their desk-drawers, and those who only consent to be read, at a pinch, by an elite, and in luxury editions. Ordinary human beings, with no reason to slam the door on our fellow-men, we do not consider that the poet's ideal should be to discourage his readers or forbid them all access.] 'Refusons de pratiquer une forme d'art réservée au *happy few*: elle nous interdirait révolte et communication.' [Let us refuse to practise a form of art reserved for the happy few: it would deny us all revolt and all communication.] Breton writes with considerable verve and much realism, but he is perhaps a little too self-consciously tough.

Principal collections: *Chair et soleil*, 1960; *Dire non*, 1964; *L'Eté des corps*, Guy Chambelland, 1968.

AIMÉ CÉSAIRE (1913–)

No doubt the greatest poet of the French language that the coloured races have yet produced. Critics point, rightly, to the vigour of his rhythms, which are, for French, particularly strong. His imagery also has extraordinary force and colour, sometimes of the 'local' kind, more often of that rather surrealistic type that strikes one as brilliant and fascinating long before one can attempt an explanation of its 'meaning'. And indeed a poem such as *Soleil serpent* is unparaphrasable: it is a hymn of joy to the sun, and succeeds by its energy, joie de vivre, and startling imagery. *La Roue* has more rational content, however: it is centrally about a loved woman's tears, and ends with the promise of consolation. Césaire's poems are moments of fierce emotion, vividly recreated.

Césaire was born in Martinique, the son of a minor official, and continued his education in Paris, where, with Senghor, he originated the notion of *négritude* and helped to found a paper called *L'Etudiant Noir* which proposed such American negro writers as Langston Hughes as literary models. After the Ecole Normale, Césaire returned to Martinique to teach (1939). About this time he met André Breton, and realized that he had been 'un peu surréaliste sans le savoir' [almost a surrealist without knowing it]. The logic of his pro-black, anti-colonial thought led to his being invited by the Communists to stand for Mayor of Fort-de-France; and, to his own amazement, he was elected. His election as deputy of Martinique followed. He left the Party in 1956 after the Hungarian Revolution, and founded his own political movement.

Principal collections: *Les armes miraculeuses*, Gallimard 1946; *Cahier d'un retour au pays natal*, Présence Africaine, 1956;

Cadastre, Seuil, 1961 (including *Soleil cou coupé*, originally published by Editions K in 1948); *Ferrements*, Seuil, 1960.

CLAUDE MICHEL CLUNY (1930–)

Claude Michel Cluny was born on 2 July 1930 near Charleville, but he has never lived there. His childhood was spent in the region of Paris, as were his studies, which he interrupted in 1950 to travel to Germany. Since 1955 he has made numerous journeys in Europe, North Africa, the Middle East and South America. In 1966 he became a literary critic on *Lettres Françaises* and began to direct a documentary service on French Radio, and in 1967 he succeeded J.-L. Curtis as film critic on *La Nouvelle Revue Française*. He has published two novels (*La balle au bond* and *Un jeune homme de Venise*) and, among other work, an anthology entitled *L'humour la poésie* (Librairie St-Germain-des-Prés, 1970).

The epigraph to *Désordres* is from Horace, and reads: 'Parmi l'espoir et le souci, entre les craintes et les colères, crois que chaque jour pour toi luit le dernier.' [Amid hope and distress, amid fear and anger, believe every day that shines to be your last.] This very modern sentiment succinctly expresses Claude Michel Cluny's philosophy. His poetry is full of the bright sunlight of places he has visited, and of dark shadows, as in the sex- and death-haunted *Racines*; and sometimes, as in the recent *Pelouse*, he achieves an elegant ironic detachment.

Collections: *Désordres*, Gallimard, 1965; *La mort sur l'épaule* (Editions Rencontre, Lausanne and Geneva, 1970).

JEAN-PAUL DE DADELSEN (1913–57)

Dadelsen spent most of his life outside France. After working as a teacher and a journalist, he was with the French Service of the BBC from 1948 onwards. He did not begin writing poetry until he was 38. In June 1957 he died of cancer of the brain, an illness which he seems to have prophesied in some of his poems. Most of his work remained unpublished till after his death.

According to Henri Thomas, in his introduction to Dadelsen's collected poems (*Jonas*, Gallimard, 1962), Dadelsen appeared very much the gay dog to his friends and colleagues. His deepest inner preoccupation, a tormented and death-obsessed search for God, was allowed voice only in his poetry.

Dadelsen is a rather garrulous poet, not at all difficult, and his tone is often ironic and slangy. He is definitely outside the main stream of French poetry since the War, and some critics have charged him with insufficient discipline. It must be remembered that his writing career was brief; and even so, his work has a quite inimitable flavour.

His only published work is *Jonas* (mentioned above), most of which has been excellently translated into English by Edward Lucie-Smith (*Jonah*, Rapp & Carroll, 1967).

MICHEL DEGUY (1930–)

Michel Deguy was born in Paris. He taught philosophy from 1953 to 1968, and at present lectures in French literature at the Vincennes branch of the University of Paris. He is a reader at the publishing house of Gallimard, a member of the committee of their critical review, and director of the little *Revue de poésie*. He has engaged in group translation of Hölderlin, Dante, Góngora, Heidegger, and others.

Of the younger poets, Michel Deguy has perhaps the greatest range, as well as the most brilliant and experimental output. His remarkable (and difficult) series of essays on the poetic process, *Actes* (1966), asserts that poetry is a mode of knowledge (non-scientific, of course): its ambiguity corresponds to the ambiguity of the world we inhabit, and everything is grist to its mill. Accordingly, Deguy's own poetry ranges from humour to philosophy, from metaphysics to the visible world. This is already apparent in an early poem like *Le golfe*: nature is an image for the poet's task: butterflies for instance are 'paper insects', and his ear to the ground records the beat of his own blood—which is also the pulse of nature. It is in *Ouï dire* ('Hearsay': a lovely title for a book of poems!) that Deguy's startling virtuosity as poet can be seen at its best: he makes his vocabulary draw on every facet of experience, even the most difficult facets of all, namely the technical or scientific, and yet achieves poetry: for one feels his most outrageous comparisons are always 'right' and exact. The final poem given here, for example, contains terms taken from gymnastics, horsemanship and fencing.

More recently, Deguy has been injecting his language with an ever larger dose of philosophy, in pursuit of what he calls the *poème sourd* ('poem in a low key', perhaps), which is neither prose nor verse, and is truly modern. Into these rarefied regions not everyone will follow him, but the fact remains that his is the contemporary poetic genius most lavishly endowed.

Collections: *Fragment du cadastre*, 1960; *Poèmes de la presqu'île*, 1961; *Biefs*, 1963; *Ouï dire*, 1966; *Figurations*, 1969 (all published by Gallimard).

ANDRÉ DU BOUCHET (1924–)

André du Bouchet was born in Paris, and at the age of seventeen went to the United States, where he remained seven years, studying at Amherst, then at Harvard, where he was Teaching Fellow in English and Comparative Literature, and obtained an M.A. in English. He returned to France in 1948. Like Bonnefoy, he has translated Shakespeare (*Pericles, Henry VIII* and *The Tempest*).

Du Bouchet's careful typographical arrangements of his poems on the page leaves blanks designed to express silence, lapses of meaning, abrupt changes and so forth; they also indicate a preoccupation with whiteness, which seems to symbolize for him the purity of the *tabula rasa*. Professor Hackett says of his work: 'he evokes a fragmentary, elemental world in which there are brusque movements, unexpected events, sudden storms and conflagrations, but also a tenacious, if erratic, human endeavour.'

Dans la chaleur vacante, published in 1961, includes most of du Bouchet's work up to that date. Since then he has published *Où le soleil*, Mercure de France, 1968.

JACQUES DUPIN (1927–)

Jacques Dupin was born on 4 March 1927 at Privas in the Ardèche. He works in a contemporary art gallery, and consequently 'lives' among painters. He is a member of the editorial committee of *L'Ephémère*, along with Michel Leiris, Yves Bonnefoy, André du Bouchet and Louis-René des Forêts. And he has never received a literary prize!

Dupin's principal collections are *Gravir*, 1963 and *L'embrasure*, 1969 (both published by Gallimard). His poetry is difficult, and reveals the influence of René Char. However, he has an admirable gift for the sharp and exact image: consider for instance the justness of a phrase like 'la lenteur d'une épissure/aux prise avec les ongles' [the slowness of a splice /at odds with the fingernails], which somehow combines both abstract and concrete in the same sensation. The four fragments here torn from *L'embrasure* come from a section entitled *La nuit grandissante* (Enlarging Night). It is a pity to have to break this sequence up, but the ambiguous 'he' of these poems stands for the poet, his inspiration, his mysterious self and alter ego. The third person is distancing (and poets usually feel that it is not 'they' who write their poems). Dupin's poetry is both cool and sharp, laconic and profoundly suggestive.

JEAN-PIERRE DUPREY (1930–59)

Duprey was a Surrealist, one of André Breton's protégés. For some years he spent more energy on painting and sculpture than on poetry, and his poetic output is small. For having committed the fully Surrealist gesture of urinating on the flame of the Unknown Soldier, Duprey was imprisoned and then transferred to a psychiatric hospital. Although no doubt not the direct cause of his end, this experience did nothing to restore him to acceptance of life, and he committed suicide shortly after his release. A few weeks before his death, he answered an inquiry after his health with the words: 'Je suis allergique à la planète.' [I'm allergic to the planet.] Suicide is of course another fully Surrealist act.

La fin et la manière is his poetic testament: it was written in a few weeks, and Duprey posted it to André Breton just before committing suicide. The poems in it are the work of a self-condemned man, unable to face the absurdity of life. Rarely can such savage wit and verbal brilliance have been used to celebrate nothingness with such verve. Duprey's language plays angrily with words and notions, takes wild leaps—but the leaps are always into the absurd, and he is left in the final resort in a no-man's-land of negatives.

Derrière son double, 1965; *La fin et la manière*, 1965 (both published by Le Soleil Noir).

JEAN FOLLAIN (1903–)

Quite outside any literary movements, Jean Follain has been ploughing his solitary furrow for a long time now, and is one of the most esteemed minor poets of his generation. Most of his life he spent as an advocate, then as a judge, in the same 'unpoetic' profession, in short, as America's Wallace Stevens!

Henri Thomas describes his chief ambition as that of 'refusing the illusion of lyricism', a formula which does not mean quite the same in French as in English. In French lyricism is often associated with explicit emotional commentary, even with sentimental gush: clearly nothing could be further from Follain's intentions. His poems are like paintings: they offer us a few selected objects, juxtaposed, as texts for meditating the strangeness of the world, its contingency, its refusal to submit to any scheme of rational control. He himself offers no comments, and is as absent from his poetry as a writer can be. Thomas also notes the absence of metaphors in Follain. Well, this is not quite true, but very nearly, and it is clear why: the strangeness and pathos of the world as it is, is always the theme of poetry; but in Follain, this theme is suggested not by the use of imagery as such, but by the juxtaposition of actual objects in the world that are not usually associated, and which then suggest either an absence of meaning or the kind of secret meaning beyond reason that only the greatest poetry can hint at.

Principal collections: *Usage du temps*, 1943; *Exister*, 1947; *Territoires*, 1953; *Tout instant*, 1957; *Des heures*, 1960; *Appareil de la terre*, 1964; *D'après tout*, 1967 (all published by Gallimard). *Exister* and *Territoires* have been collected together in the series Poésie Gallimard, 1969.

ANDRÉ FRÉNAUD (1907-)

André Frénaud is a Burgundian (which is why, in *Autoportrait*, he rolls his r's), born between slagheaps and vineyards. Most of his life he worked with the French Railways, but has now retired.

Frénaud, like Follain, is an enemy of gush and rhetoric, but is present in many of his poems as an ironic observer, or behind some persona such as that of the Three Magi. Irony, tenderness, and a laconic, tough and often slangy use of language are the hallmarks of Frénaud's style. His most recurrent theme is that of the absence of God, and his attitude to metaphysical questions is in some ways comparable with that of Albert Camus. Christian myth is thus turned to his own uses in such poems as *Les Rois Mages*, where the search for a Saviour has clearly been going on for close on two thousand years, the star is a dream, and the Three Kings were misdirected from the start. Yet our metaphysical thirst is real, though there is no way of satisfying it. This is all far from negative, for Frénaud draws a stoical courage from Man's impossible situation, and a value from the hopeless search for value.

Frénaud's poetry is particularly powerful and robust. It contains both sensuous surface and metaphysical depth, and skilfully harmonizes a considerable variety of tones.

Most of Frénaud's poetry is collected in the four volumes, *Les Rois Mages*, Seghers, 1943 (republished 1966); *Il n'y a pas de paradis*, Gallimard, 1962 (republished 1967); *La Sainte Face*, Gallimard, 1968; *Depuis toujours déjà*, Gallimard 1970.

JACQUES GARELLI (1935–)

Jacques Garelli has studied literature and philosophy, and has worked for UNESCO, teaching French literature in Congo-Kinshasa and Madagascar. He is the author of one of the most interesting theoretical works on poetry to appear since the war, namely *La gravitation poétique* (Mercure de France, 1966). The opening chapters of this work present some difficulty to the British reader not versed in Continental philosophy, since they attempt to relate the doctrines of Existentialism and Phenomenology to the 'truth' of poetry. Poetry, in Garelli's view, is a moment-by-moment record of existence, as it 'surges' into being. As one might perhaps have expected, Garelli is fascinated by Rimbaud and by Surrealist automatic writing, which he regards as an authentic picture of the world's 'coming-to-be'. The poem *Annexion*, given here, is a statement of this *ars poetica*, and one should note the existentialist term *fonde* (founds) in the first paragraph. The word means, approximately, 'creates, asserts and validates existence'.

Garelli lays extraordinary reliance upon the ability of sounds to suggest meaning. It is notorious that such interpretations are at the mercy of the interpreter's subjectivity, and this attitude of Garelli's explains the hermetic obscurity of his poetry. He has as yet however produced only two slim volumes, *Brèche*, 1966, and *Les dépossessions*, 1968 (both published by Mercure de France).

ROGER GIROUX (1925–)

Roger Giroux was born at Lyon, and holds a degree in English. He has translated a number of Lawrence Durrell's novels into French, including the *Alexandria Quartet*; and also Yeats's play *The Herne's Egg*. He worked on the Série Noire, a collection of crime novels published by Gallimard. He received the Prix Max-Jacob for his collection *L'arbre le temps* (Mercure de France, 1964).

Giroux has written little, and his poems often describe the struggle to spin words out of silence, to express the inexpressible. Appropriately, the first section of *L'arbre le temps* is entitled *Retrouver la parole* (To reconquer speech). 'Rien n'est jamais dit et toujours dire ce rien: telle est la perpétuelle naissance du poète,' writes Giroux. [Nothing is ever said, and always to say this nothing: such is the poet's continual re-birth.]

JEAN PAUL GUIBBERT (1942–)

Jean Paul Guibbert was born at Béziers on 30 August 1942, and baptized at the Church of St Aphrodise, in an early Christian sarcophagus—which could be taken as a symbol of certain recurrent themes in his work. For instance there is a pre-occupation with death, particularly in his earlier work, and a perfectionism explicable by his ambition to live and write 'in function of his death', polishing each poetic gesture as if it were his last. The poems of *Alyscamps* are variations on the theme of love and death: 'Béatrice' is at once a remembered mistress, a present Muse (like Dante's Beatrice), and a figure who combines the temptations of Eros and mortality. (Alyscamps itself is of course the famous early Christian cemetery at Arles.) Guibbert's most recent work has become much more hermetic, a fact which can be accounted for by his personal hunt for a crystalline hardness and perfection. Similar preoccupations can be observed, however: the jade-like fragility of a woman is evoked in *Jade*; and the silence in the final poem given here can stand for both normal failures of communication, even between lovers, and that final failure of all contact, namely death.

Collections of poetry since 1966: *Alyscamps*, Mercure de France, 1966; *Arc*, LCL, 1966 (ill. by Alain Clément); *Mémoire*, Bernard Astruc (publisher), 1967 (ill. by Alain Clément); *OE*, Fata Maorgana, 1968 (ill. by Alain Clément); *13 poèmes d'un âge cœur*, LEO, 1969; *Verticale rose et soie rayée*, Pathmos, 1970 (ill. by Patrice Vermeille).

GUILLEVIC (1907–)

Guillevic was born at Carnac, in Brittany, but never learned the Breton language. He settled in Paris in 1935, and spent most of his working life as a Civil Servant in various govern-ment ministries. He joined the Communist Party during the War, and was a friend of Paul Eluard. *Gagner* (1949) suffers, in the view of the majority of critics, from its political *engage-ment*, but Guillevic has since returned to his previous manner.

His poetry is slight, delicate, pure and genuine. He communicates the authentic poetic thrill, and achieves this with the slightest of touches. His work has the same kind of small-scale perfection as the *haiku*.

Principal collections: *Terraqué* and *Exécutoire* (1942 and 1947. Both republished in one volume by Gallimard, 1968); *Gagner*, 1949; *Carnac*, 1961; *Sphère*, 1963; *Avec*, 1966; *Euclidiennes*, 1967; *Ville*, 1969 (all published by Gallimard).

ANNE HÉBERT (1916–)

Anne Hébert is perhaps French Canada's finest poet. She was born at Sainte-Catherine de Fossambault, a village of 1000 inhabitants, about twenty miles west of Quebec, and lived most of her early life at Quebec itself. Her father Maurice Hébert was a critic and propagandist for French Canadian letters between the wars. The classical purism of her father's outlook manifests itself however in an utterly different way in Anne Hébert's own work: Pierre Emmanuel says of her poems that they 'seem incised in bone by the point of a dagger', a remark which emphasizes their hard metallic quality, their compression, and the painful quality of much of the imagery. With her cousin Saint-Denys Garneau (a tragic figure who died at the age of 31), Anne Hébert is one of the founders of modern Québecois poetry.

Principal collections: *Les songes en équilibre*, Montréal, 1942; *Le tombeau des rois*, Québec, 1953; *Poèmes*, Seuil, 1960. See also *Anne Hébert*, by René Lacôte, Poètes d'aujourd'hui, Seghers, 1969.

PHILIPPE JACCOTTET (1925–)

Born in Switzerland, in the Canton of Vaud, Jaccottet now lives in a little village in the hills of the Drôme. There is a radical change from his early manner (that of *L'effraie*) to his later (for instance *Airs*). In *L'effraie* he writes poems in practically traditional form and style. In *Airs*, the poems are in a sense the same poems, but shortened, all elements of exposition or explanation removed from them. It seems that between the two, Jaccottet was influenced by the Japanese *haiku*, and the gain in his poetry is visible: the poems of *Airs* are disturbing, without one being able to lay one's finger too firmly upon their 'subjects'. One is therefore forced (in classic modern style) to think through the imagery to the meaning. In *Tout à la fin de la nuit* the clue is Charon, the ferryman of Hades. *Toute fleur n'est que de la nuit* is about the reality behind reality: to pretend to name this would be but to pretend. Jaccottet's poetry is perhaps slight, but communicates the authentic *frisson*.

Principal collections: *L'effraie*, 1958; *L'ignorant*, 1958; *Airs*, 1967 (all published by Gallimard); *Leçons*, Payot, Lausanne, 1969.

JEAN JOUBERT (1928–)

Jean Joubert was born on 27 February 1928 at Chalette-sur-Loing, near Montargis, studied English at the Sorbonne, and has spent considerable periods in Germany, England and the United States. He at present teaches American literature at Montpellier University, and lives with his family some 14 kilometres from Montpellier in a *mas* (or farmhouse typical of the region). Joubert admits to some influence by Éluard and the Surrealists, but the symbols in his poetry are often used more in the manner of another of his influences, Yeats, and can be related to outer, as well as inner, reality. He has also written two novels (*Les neiges de juillet* and *La forêt blanche*).

Poetry: *Les lignes de la main*, Seghers, 1955; *Poèmes d'absence*, Gallimard, 1959; *Campagnes secrètes*, Cahiers de la Licorne, 1963; *Oniriques*, LEO, 1964; *Neuf poèmes immobiles*, LEO, 1968; *Corps désarmé à la merci des arbres*, Guy Chambelland, 1969.

JEAN LAUDE (1922–)

Jean Laude was born at Dunkirk, and holds a degree in French literature. He works at the Musée de l'Homme. During the War he was deported to Germany for forced labour.

Many of the poets of Laude's generation specialize in *dépouillement* (the fining down of the poem's imagery to its bare essentials), but in none is the effect so deliberately grey and muted. Laude describes scenes that never were in heaven or earth, but perhaps may be in limbo. This poetry inhabits the beaches of Ultima Thule (the title after all of one of his collections). Each poem is built up slowly out of numerous repetitions, which accurately suggest the obsessiveness of the situation, and which somehow avoid any effect of precise definition: the picture does not become 'clearer'. The subject is Man's situation seen as utterly solitary, facing northward into the cold mist of an Otherwhere. The monotony is intentional. It is perhaps a narrowing of poetic range to confine one-self to one end only of the gamut of experience that runs from the immediate fact to the ultimate metaphysical uncertainty; but within his limits Laude is a hauntingly successful 'psychological' poet.

Collections: *Entre deux morts*, G.L.M., 1947; *Le grand passage*, Editions du Dragon, 1955; *Les saisons et la mer*, Seuil, 1959; *Les plages de Thulé*, Seuil, 1964.

ARMEN LUBIN (1903–)

Armen Lubin, after a happy childhood followed by exile from his native Armenia, had to spend many years in hospitals and sanatoriums. His poetry faces illness and fear with a touching courage and wry humour. He uses approximately traditional rimes and metres, but his rhythms are halting—the equivalent in sound of the hesitant ironies of his imagery. His poetry is no doubt slight, but has entirely individual tone.

Collections: *Le passager clandestin*, 1946; *Sainte patience*, 1951; *Transfert nocturne*, 1955; *Les hautes terrasses*, 1957 (all four published by Gallimard); *Feux contre feux*, Grasset, 1968 (which constitutes in effect Lubin's Selected Poems).

JOYCE MANSOUR (1928–)

Joyce Mansour was born in England of Egyptian parents, and is a leading member of the post-war Surrealist Movement. Her poetry is limited in scope, but individual, and by no means as difficult as the label 'Surrealist' might lead one to suppose. I include her for her quite individual note of feline savagery.

Her poetry is collected in *Rapaces* (Seghers, 1960).

ROBERT MARTEAU (1925–   )

Robert Marteau was born on 8 February 1925 in a village in Poitou not far from Dampierre-sur-Boutonne, the castle associated with alchemy. He studied at Niort till the age of 18, when he went to Paris; and he has divided his time between Paris, Poitou and the Pyrenees, and spent long summers in Spain, for he is an *aficionado* of the bull-ring. He has translated Góngora, and the Yugoslav poet Pavlović. He is deeply involved in the visual arts, is responsible for organizing exhibitions, and is currently preparing a film in Yugoslavia on Byzantine frescoes, and a book on the stained glass of Chagall.

Much of Marteau's imagery is drawn from myth, as witness the sections given here from his long poem *Travaux pour un bûcher*. Death cannot be exorcized, of course, but it is as if the myth of the phoenix, for example, or of the pharaonic sun-god, speak consolingly to the collective unconscious. Despite the consequence that the subjects of his poetry are the great elemental themes, Marteau's language has a concreteness and specificity unusual in French, and this gives his poetry a particularly savorous and vital quality.

Principal collections: *Royaumes*, Seuil, 1962; *Travaux sur la terre*, Seuil, 1966. A further book of his poems is due shortly.

FERNAND OUELLETTE (1930–)

Fernand Ouellette was born at Montréal on 24 September 1930. He has received prizes for his work from the Canadian Arts Council, from the Quebec Ministry for Cultural Affairs, and the Prix France-Québec for his biography of the composer Edgar Varèse. He was co-founder and, since 1961, has been editor of the Canadian French language review *Liberté*. Between 1966 and 1968 he was on the Commission of Inquiry set up by the Government of Quebec into the Teaching of the Arts, and is a co-author of their 3-volume report, which represents a great step forward in educational thinking, as it proposes to base the educational system on creativity and artistic training. Various essays of his have appeared in *Liberté* over the years on such subjects as bilingualism, the linguistic situation of Quebec, the poetry of T. S. Eliot and Pierre Jean Jouve. He works as a producer for Radio Canada, where he concerns himself with cultural broadcasts; and he wrote the poetry and scenario for a cantata entitled *Psaumes pour abri* in collaboration with the composer Pierre Mercure, in 1963.

His collection *Le soleil sous la mort* speaks for a world lying under threat of an atomic holocaust. The poems here included are, however, all taken from *Dans le sombre*, his densest and profoundest work to date. In this highly Freudian poetry, the influence of Jouve is evident. Unlike Jouve's poetry, however, Ouellette's is not concerned with the power of the impulses of Eros and Thanatos to save Man in a Christian sense, but to reveal his preconscious, pagan and archetypal impulses. The imagery is compact and violent; there is a frequent use of the adjective as substantive, which in the original French leads on the one hand to increased concreteness, on the other to a heightening of the tone. Ouellette's language achieves an extraordinary blend of the blatantly sexual and of a tone loftier even than Jouve's: the effect is to celebrate and hallow the sex-instinct and the love-relationship, and give them the quality of a solemn rite.

Poetry: *Ces anges de sang*, 1955; *Séquences de l'aile*, 1958; *Le soleil sous la mort*, 1965; *Dans le sombre*, 1967 (all published by L'Hexagone, Montreal).

JEAN PÉROL (1932–)

Jean Pérol was born on 19 May 1932 at Vienne, and it is in the South-East of France that he prefers to live (when in France). Some of his memories are haunted, since this region of France passed through fire and the sword in the years of the Resistance. A poetry incapable of assimilating and expressing violence is thus entirely foreign to Pérol, would for him be incapable of expressing twentieth-century experience. And he admires above all Henri Michaux's unconventional, subversive and disturbing rejection of the merely literary. The great experience in Pérol's life, however, is undoubtedly his stay in Japan (1961–8; and he has recently returned there), which taught him, he says, that poetry is not about ephemera (such as politics), but only about those ephemera which are eternal (such as *Les flagelles d'avril*).

Le cœur véhément was chosen as a title because it would displease. The collection itself, like his next volume, *Ruptures*, has an architecture, is deliberately organized. Although *Le coeur véhément* is largely set, and was written, in Japan, it contains no 'exoticism' (which would be merely decoration, permitting the writer and reader an easy escape to regions where one's emotions are not engaged), but is an attempt to record the clash of images and meanings set up in a poet's mind when his own cultural heritage is to some extent invaded by another. Such a poem as *Kikou* illustrates how revealing this can be: the chrysanthemum stands for death in the West, for love in the East: the two images are both explored, and their amalgamation offers a deeper sense. The poems of *Le coeur véhément* are in prose, since they record a meeting of cultures, and context had to be given them. *Ruptures* is partly in prose, partly in verse, but I have thought it best to familiarize the reader with Pérol's prose poetry here: and it *is* clearly a fine poetry, vehement in rhythm, glowing with images, and instinct with life.

Principal collections: *L'atelier*, Guy Chambelland, 1961; *Le point vélique*, Guy Chambelland, 1965; *D'un pays lointain*, Shichôsha, Tokyo, 1965; *Le coeur véhément*, Gallimard, 1968;

Ruptures, Gallimard, 1970.

ANDRÉ PIEYRE DE MANDIARGUES (1909–)

André Pieyre de Mandiargues' family background is a mixture of Norman, Mediterranean and Calvinist. His first book *Dans les années sordides* was published at Monte Carlo, where he took refuge during the War. He has been associated with the Surrealists since 1947, and has a strong affinity with their attitudes.

Le chasseur appears in *Le point où j'en suis*, Gallimard, 1964. A selection of his work can be found in *L'âge de craie*, Gallimard, 1967.

RAYMOND QUENEAU (1903–)

Queneau was born in Le Havre, and obtained a degree in philosophy. He then did various odd jobs before deciding to be a writer. He was an active member of the Surrealist Movement between 1924 and 1930, one of his actions being the writing of the pamphlet *Permettez!* attacking the citizens of Charleville, on the occasion of their unveiling of a statue to Rimbaud, for having never understood the poet, and for representing all that Rimbaud himself detested most. He wrote his first novel *Le chiendent* in 1933, and has since become widely known in France and abroad for his novels, in which comic absurdity is used to convey tragic absurdity. He is now literary director of the publishing house of Gallimard.

Queneau is above all an anti-poet, who has enormous linguistic energy and virtuosity. His jokes betray intelligence masquerading (but not always) as stupidity. His output of poetry is enormous but its effects are limited. However, I must confess to an especial soft spot for the vulgarities of his *Art poétique*!

Les Ziaux, 1943; *Bucoliques*, 1947; *L'instant fatal*, 1948; *Petite cosmogonie portative*, 1950; *Si tu t'imagines*, 1952; *Le chien à la mandoline*, 1958; *Cent mille millards de poèmes*, 1958; *Courir les rues*, 1967; *Battre la campagne*, 1968; *Fendre les flots*, 1969 (all published by Gallimard).

JEAN-JOSEPH RABÉARIVELO (1903–37)

Rabéarivelo was born at Antananarivo in Madagascar, and left school at the age of 12, becoming in turn secretary and translator to a cantonal chief, errand-boy to a scrap-dealer, and librarian. After a period without fixed employment he became proof-reader in a printing firm, though he received no payment until two years after he had joined them. In this same year (1926) he married. His appetite for French literature was voracious, and his knowledge of it entirely self-taught. The great tragedy of his life was the death of his daughter Voahangy in October 1933, a death that he attributed to the incompetence and malice of the local medical authorities. He instituted what seems to have been almost a cult to her memory. His salary was tiny, his expenses on his family and on his books enormous, his attempts to enter the Administration (which would have solved his financial problems) without success. Pursued by creditors, and receiving on 20 June 1937 a final refusal from the Administration, he committed suicide two days later.

Rabéarivelo's work is French by its language, Malagasy by its inspiration. It is of the purest poetry, as I should judge, by the fact that the poems here included conform to Robert Graves's criterion—that they produce the genuine cold shiver denoting (says Graves) the passage of the Muse.

Principal works: see the Anthology published by Nathan, Paris, 1967; also *Poèmes, Presque-Songes, Traduit de la nuit, Saiky-Nofy* (2nd edition), Antananarivo, 1960.

JACQUES RÉDA (1929–)

Jacques Réda was born on 24 January 1929 at Lunéville, in Lorraine, but has lived since 1938 in or near Paris. He has written for the *Cahiers du Sud*, the *Nouvelle Revue Française* and the *Cahiers du Chemin*, and worked as a critic on *Jazz Magazine* for some years. Although he has always written poetry, he regards the volume from which the poems published here are taken, namely *Amen* (1968), as his first 'real' collection. It was followed in 1970 by *Récitatif*. (Both are published by Gallimard.)

The relative clarity of Réda's work assists the deeply poetic effect of such details as Trotsky's last minute catching of his spectacles in *Matin d'Octobre* and their smashing at the end of the poem—or the leaping of years in the middle of a sentence that occurs in the same poem. Réda has an original way with his images, which build slowly, deepening and transforming themselves as they do so; this involves him in long winding sentences, whose balance and rhythm he controls perfectly. From both these points of view he is a highly interesting and original poet. The total effect of his poems is certainly more than the sum of their parts, and his is perhaps the most profound poetry recently published in France.

JEAN-CLAUDE RENARD (1922-)

Jean-Claude Renard's early poetry was, as with many French Catholic poets in this century, largely traditional in form. Around 1965, however, there came a complete change in his approach, and the poems of his two most recent volumes, *La terre du sacre* and *La braise et la rivière*, are at once more modern, more difficult and more disciplined than anything he had written previously. To this new difficulty of expression corresponds a new difficulty of belief: in *La terre du sacre*, writes its author, 'plus rien (ou presque) n'est affirmé, proclamé avec l'assurance de la certitude, mais . . . presque tout, au contraire, semble remis en question et rendu à une sorte de nuit originelle, pour ne pas dire de négation, de "point zéro" primordial . . .' [nothing—or almost nothing—is affirmed any longer, or proclaimed with an assurance of certainty, but, on the contrary, almost everything seems to be called once again in question, to be cast back into a sort of primeval night, not to say negation or primordial zero point . . .][1] And he notes that 'on dirait que ce que nous appelons Dieu se taît, s'anéantit, nous laisse dans l'abandon et dans la solitude pour qu'affranchis de tout ce qui nous serait imposé de l'extérieur . . . nous devenions capables d'atteindre et d'expérimenter librement ce qu'il y a en nous de fondamentalement fait pour le divin . . .' [it is as if what we call God is becoming silence and nothingness, is leaving us abandoned and alone so that, freed from anything that might be imposed upon us from without . . ., we may become capable of achieving and experiencing freely whatever in us is basically made for the divine . . .] Renard's poetry is in fact the first to adopt the position of the 'Death of God' theologians; and in this new admission of the difficulty of finding God, he has finally found his true poetic voice. I suspect that it is the sincerities of poetry that have led him to this point: for the certainties of strict form have been abandoned along with the certainties of faith.

As so often in contemporary French poetry, Renard's language concentrates not on sensuous detail, but on simple basic words (tree, fire, wind) which have to be almost

[1] This and the next quotation can be found on p. 146 of *Notes sur la poésie*, Jean-Claude Renard, 1970.

'translated' mentally. The wind in *Si l'arbre prenait nom* suggests a wind from God, a divine message; the tree reminds of the crucifixion, suggests Christ; the birds suggest the doves of grace. It is as if narrow senses have been translated into broad vague words. But the vagueness is necessary: for God and Christ have question-marks attached to them; and it is now Renard's business to suggest our need of, and potentiality for, the divine only through an intimation of its absence. At the same time, there is a considerable lyrical impulse in Renard, and it is a measure of his quality as a poet that he controls it with such firmness. He is one of France's finest contemporary poets.

Collections: *Juan*, Paris, Editions M. Didier, 1945; *Cantiques pour des pays perdus*, 1947, Robert Laffont, Paris, and 1957, Points et Contrepoints, Paris; *Métamorphose du monde*, Points et Contrepoints, 1951; *Fable*, Seghers, 1952; *Père, voici que l'homme*, Seuil, 1955; *En une seule vigne*, Seuil, 1959; *Incantation des eaux*, Points et Contrepoints, 1961; *Incantation du temps*, Seuil, 1962; *La terre du sacre*, Seuil, 1966; *La braise et la rivière*, Seuil, 1969. See also his meditations on poetry, *Notes sur la poésie*, Seuil, 1970.

DENIS ROCHE (1937–)

Denis Roche's observations on poetry (see for instance the introduction to *Eros énergumène*) seem to me more convincing than his actual poems. Naturally, however, there is a connexion. He demands that poetry should be relieved of all moral, emotional, sentimental and philosophical indices. This is in effect simply a demand for extreme 'objectivity', and since such objectivity has been a constant concern of modern poets, it might be thought that Roche is not saying anything new. But one should note the extremism of the statement: it is a *total* abolition of emotional indices, of any overt attitude whatever, that he is recommending. He notes that there is a 'gesture' in any written production, but that this gesture should betray itself only by its absence. Hence his *Eros énergumène*, endlessly producing in a state of emotionless frenzy. But this is negative, and indeed Roche has nothing positive to say except that writing and reading imply each other and are social acts. But signifying what? Without significance there can be no choice: one might as well read *anything*!

It will be clear that Denis Roche's poetry is an extreme

antipoetry. By the arbitrary imposition of formless forms upon his 'poems', he seeks to destroy all accepted notions of 'poetry'. This is why he says, 'La poésie est inadmissible.' [Poetry is inadmissible.] What are we left with? He says he has 'deux volontés: celle du formaliste et celle du poseur de mines.' [Two intentions: to be a formalist, and to lay booby-traps.] It could be said of course that this is a valid metaphor for experience. But if it remains merely basic, and if the details of that experience are of insufficient interest, it cannot reproduce experience—which, whatever else one says of it, is at least interesting! Where then does the interest in Roche reside? In the wittiness of his games with form (as in the anticalligram given here); and in the charming playfulness of some of his more erotic 'poems'.

Collections: *Récits complets*, Seuil, 1963; *Les idées centésimales de Miss Elanize*, Seuil, 1964; *Éros énergumène*, Seuil, 1968. Denis Roche has also translated Pound's *Pisan Cantos* and *ABC of Reading* into French.

JACQUES ROUBAUD (1932–)

Jacques Roubaud was born on 5 December 1932. His profession is mathematics, which he teaches at the University of Nanterre. He tells me that in his view mathematics and poetry are two equal (and opposite) modes of understanding. He has published 'imitations' (à la Lowell) of early Japanese lyrical poems, and has collaborated with three other poets writing in Spanish, English and Italian respectively, on a multilingual poem.

ε, from which the poems given here are taken, is a set of variations on the sonnet form. The riming sonnets (of various forms and kinds) are there to destroy the validity of the form at least in so far as Roubaud himself is concerned, by means of a highly arbitrary (but dazzling and apt) choice of words—arbitrary because chosen by the form rather than by the poet. As for the form of the book as a whole, this too is arbitrary: the plan of a game of Go is set out at the end of it, and most of the poems bear the number of a move in the game. Certain of the poems are supposed to be arranged in patterns corresponding to certain patterns of the Go counters. The fiction of the Go game is in part (as the preface explains) a way of indicating that there are many different orders in which the poems of a collection may be read. But it is also a metaphor for poetry (black letter against white space), the conquest of silence (ditto), life and death (white versus black), etc. And to the extent that it is a gimmick (which it clearly also is), it is at least an extremely elegant one.

All the poems given here except *Ennemie* are 'prose sonnets' taken from groups of 'sonnets of sonnets'. (A sonnet of sonnets contains of course fourteen sonnets—and three blank spaces.) As so often in ε, Roubaud's technique here tends towards the fragmentary: he builds his effects up almost like a pointillist, image upon disconnected image; and even the syntax of his sentences tends to break up. The effect is of a dilapidation—which *builds*.

Collections: ε, Gallimard, 1967; *Le sentiment des choses*, Gallimard, 1970; *Renga* (in collaboration with three other poets), Gallimard, 1970.

JEAN-PHILIPPE SALABREUIL (1940–70)

Jean-Pierre Steinbach, who published under the name of Jean-Philippe Salabreuil, was born at Neuilly-sur-Seine. He studied Law and Literature. He published his first poems in *Les Cahiers des Saisons* and in *La Nouvelle Revue Française*. His first book, *La Liberté des feuilles*, whose title is taken from a line by René-Guy Cadou, appeared in 1963. His second, *Juste retour d'abîme* (1965), is less lyrical and more haunted, and documents a return to life after a kind of dark night of the mind. Salabreuil spent two years in Congo-Kinshasa under the aegis of aid to underdeveloped countries, and published a third book, *L'inespéré* in 1969. In this same year he joined the Research Service of French Radio. He died tragically in Paris at the age of 30.

Salabreuil's delicate rimes and rhythms clearly echo an almost painful sensitivity: he seems a poet easily wounded and tempted by despair. But there is no sentimentality here: the pathos has a pure and genuine, sometimes bewildered, simplicity. His world is almost unpeopled, a world of strange silence and solitude confronting the night. Its landscapes resemble those of certain kinds of dream: they contain few, but significant, objects, and colours as primary as symbols.

His three collections, mentioned above, are all published by Gallimard. A handful of posthumous poems can be found in *La Nouvelle Revue Française* and *Les Cahiers du Chemin*.

JUDE STÉFAN (1936–)

Jude Stéfan was born at Pont-Audemer in the Eure, and his profession is the teaching of literature. He has so far published *Cyprès* and *Libères* (1967 and 1970 respectively, both with Gallimard). These collections show increasing concentrated power, a violence bursting through the formality of language and constriction of scale (all his poems are as brief as the examples given). A good deal of Stéfan's force seems to be obtained by the constricting of his verse not merely into the limits of a few lines, but, within the line, its further compression into what appear to be truncated alexandrines. His arbitrary fracturing of words in the middle forms a part of this technique—perhaps the most dubious part, but there is no denying that he usually achieves a painful and intense heightening of small fragments of experience.

JEAN TARDIEU (1903–)

Jean Tardieu was born at Saint-Germain de Joux in the Jura, was educated in Paris at the Lycée Condorcet and then at the Sorbonne. He was on the staff of the National Museums, then of the publisher Hachette, took part in the Resistance during the Occupation, and joined French Radio after the War. He is an important dramatist of the absurd, and his exercises in this style date from 1946. He has also translated Goethe and Hölderlin.

Much of his poetry belongs to the anti-poetic tradition of Jarry, as does that of Queneau, but Tardieu's work is more varied in tone and more genuinely disturbing in effect than most of the Pataphysicians, and can be taken as seriously as indeed all true humour deserves.

See particularly *Choix de poèmes (1924–54)*, Gallimard, 1961; *Le fleuve caché (Poésies 1938–61)*, Gallimard, 1968; and *Les portes de toile*, Gallimard, 1969. The last contains a series, not so much of poetic descriptions as of brief linguistic equivalents for the worlds of painters like Corot, De Staël, Kandinsky, and musicians like Ravel or Debussy.

PIERRE TORREILLES (1921–)

Pierre Torreilles was born on 21 May 1921 in the Camargue. He studied literature and theology, was (like his friend René Char) a member of the maquis during the Occupation, and at present lives in Montpellier. His poetry has an atmosphere of light and emptiness. *Viens* seems to equate, on either side of a dazzling Mediterranean day which symbolizes life, the twin oblivions of birth and death. *Le retour* evokes a mysterious divine presence, again with suggestions of the unity of opposites.

Collections: *Noces d'Ea et Ninki*, La Baconnière, 1950; *Solve et coagula*, G.L.M., 1953; *L'Arrière pays clos*, G.L.M., 1961; *Repons*, G.L.M., 1963; *Corps dispersé d'Orphée*, La Baconnière, 1963; *Mesure de la terre*, G.L.M., 1966; *Voir*, Seuil, 1968.

Acknowledgments

The Edinburgh University Press is grateful to the following publishers for permission to reproduce the poems included in this volume: Editions Gallimard, Paris; Editions Seghers, Paris; Editions Bernard Grasset, Paris; Mercure de France, Paris; Fernand Nathan, Paris; Le Soleil Noir, Paris; Guy Chambelland, Paris; Editions L E O, Montpellier; Editions de L'Hexagone, Montreal; Editions Rencontre, Lausanne; also to Rapp & Whiting (André Deutsch), London, who hold the English language copyright in the poems by Jean-Paul de Dadelsen. The publishers acknowledge the generosity of the individual poets who agreed to their work being reproduced in this volume.